Wooden Spoon

Rugby's charity supporting disadvantaged children and young people

WOODEN SPOON

RUGBY**WORLD**'05

Editor
Ian Robertson

Photographs

Getty Images
and Colorsport

Queen Anne Press

A QUEEN ANNE PRESS BOOK

© Lennard Associates Limited 2004

First published in 2004 by
Queen Anne Press, a division of
Lennard Associates Limited
Mackerye End
Harpenden, Herts AL5 5DR

A catalogue entry is available from the British Library

ISBN 1 85291 657 5 (paperback)
ISBN 1 85291 658 3 (hardback)

Production Editor: Chris Marshall
Cover Design/Design Consultant: Paul Cooper
Printed and bound in Slovenia

The publishers would like to thank Colorsport and Getty Images for providing most of the photographs for this book.

The publishers would also like to thank David Gibson (Fotosport), Inphopics, Pat Sayer (Frontrow Photography), Chris Thau and Worcester RFC for additional material.

Contents

Foreword by HRH The Princess Royal   7

Wooden Spoon Society   8

COMMENT & FEATURES
What Now for Martin Johnson? (Martin Johnson)   16
Fortunam Velut Tunicam ... (Paul Stephens)   20
What People Want: the 2005 Lions to New Zealand (Mick Cleary)   25
Lawrence Dallaglio: a Year to Remember (Stephen Jones)   30
Henry & Jones: Directing the Action (Raechelle Edwards)   36
Young Guns: ACT's Rising Stars (Raechelle Edwards)   40

INTERNATIONAL SCENE
Rugby at its Best: International Sevens (Nigel Starmer-Smith)   48
Future Perfect: IRB Under 21 World Championship (Alan Lorimer)   54
A Game to Remember: the 1924 Olympic Rugby Final (Chris Thau)   59
Rugby Without Frontiers: the Game in Africa (Chris Thau)   63
Summer Tours 2004:
    England in New Zealand and Australia (David Hands)   67
    The Churchill Cup (Terry Cooper)   71
    Scotland in Samoa and Australia (Jill Douglas)   75
    Wales in Argentina and South Africa (Graham Clutton)   78
    Ireland in South Africa (Sean Diffley)   81

HOME FRONT
Duckworth's Dream: Worcester in the Premiership (Alastair Hignell)   86
Bath Denied: the 2003-04 Zurich Championship (Chris Hewett)   90
The Falcons Strike: the 2004 Powergen Cup Final (Alastair Hignell)   96
Wasps Bring Home the Big One: the 2003-04 Heineken Cup (Chris Jones)   100
Quins' New Love Affair: the 2004 Parker Pen Cup Final (Terry Cooper)   107

REVIEW OF THE SEASON 2003-04
England Eclipsed: the 2004 Six Nations Championship (Chris Jones)   112
The Club Scene:
    England: (Bill Mitchell)   117
    Scotland: (Alan Lorimer)   122
    Wales: (David Stewart)   126
    Ireland: (Sean Diffley)   131
    France: (Chris Thau)   134
    Italy: (Chris Thau)   136
A Summary of the Season 2003-04 (Bill Mitchell)   138

PREVIEW OF THE SEASON 2004-05
Key Players 2004-05 (Ian Robertson)   150
Fixtures 2004-05   156

Powergen is proud to support all levels of English club rugby

powergen.co.uk

FOREWORD

by HRH THE PRINCESS ROYAL

BUCKINGHAM PALACE

HRH The Princess Royal
Royal Patron
of Wooden Spoon

As Patron of the Wooden Spoon Society, it again gives me great pleasure to write the foreword to this book which continues to reflect the close association Wooden Spoon has with the game of rugby. The success of the England team at the 2003 Rugby World Cup resulted in a surge of interest in the game throughout the United Kingdom and Ireland. In a year dominated by other major sporting events such as Euro 2004 and the Olympics, the challenge for rugby is to retain and build on that interest.

Rugby is a game that demands great commitment and reserves of energy, enthusiasm and skill that are translated into a physically demanding and invariably exciting spectacle. Increasingly, these attributes are also required in the promotion and administration of the game. In today's tough economic climate, I am delighted to say that the members and supporters of Wooden Spoon bring the same attributes to their fundraising for the benefit of others, with the result that the Charity continues to flourish.

Wooden Spoon has just enjoyed a record fundraising year enabling over 40 projects to be supported - more than the Charity was able to support in its first decade. I congratulate the staff, volunteers, trustees, supporters from the business community and all the individual members who support Spoon and continue to improve the lives of disadvantaged children in the UK and Ireland.

Please enjoy this book but also support the Charity which created it and extend your enjoyment beyond these pages and into the work of Wooden Spoon.

Anne

Wooden Spoon

Rugby's charity supporting disadvantaged children and young people

Twenty-One Years Old: Spoon Officially Comes of Age

Royal Patron: HRH The Princess Royal
Patrons: Rugby Football Union • Scottish Rugby Union
                        Welsh Rugby Union • Irish Rugby Football Union

Most charities are born out of necessity – a human response to a human need. Whether it was Thomas Barnardo's intervention in the plight of poor children in London in the 1860s or Sir Bob Geldof's equally effective riposte to the famine in Ethiopia in 1984. Not so with Wooden Spoon. Spoon owes its origins to the outcome of a rugby match!

A wonderful and enduring legacy emerged in 1983 after England's rugby team were defeated by the Irish. Drowning their sorrows in a Dublin bar, the English fans were presented with a wooden spoon by the victorious Irish to symbolise a winless Five Nations Championship. Down but not out, they decided to raise their spirits by organising a spot of fund-raising for a local school. To their astonishment they raised an impressive £8,500, and a new charity – Wooden Spoon – was born.

The 'Spoon' has since distributed £8.5 million to help support children and young people challenged by mental, social and physical disadvantages. The charity has nearly 10,000 members and an impressive list of corporate supporters. At the present time, we are engaged in the funding of 40 projects throughout the UK and Ireland, more than the sum total of our work in the first decade, such is the pace of growth.

The origins of a charity more often than not will set the tone for the future. Spoon's guiding principle throughout the past 20 years has been 'to have fun while fund-raising'. This principle has seen the charity achieve tremendous success in a short time.

There are over 160,000 charities in the UK all raising funds for their chosen cause, and by any standards most would be worthy of the pound in our pockets. Collectively, their income is around £27 billion. Only 3,638, a little over two per cent, have an income level greater than £1 million. Wooden Spoon, by virtue of total annual income, is firmly placed within the United Kingdom's top 250 charities. This is a remarkable achievement in a short space of time. Our funding has contributed to 120 projects throughout the UK, having a direct impact on the lives of over 300,000 children and their families.

Wooden Spoon clearly has some unique characteristics in its origins, but also in its methods and the broad scope of its work. The charity is not restricted to one cause. Our goal, and indeed mission, is to embrace the problems of children and young people throughout the UK and Ireland who are challenged either physically, mentally or socially. Our preferred approach is to support others in the delivery of services by funding predominantly capital projects that have lasting impact.

Looking to the future, we decided to take stock, absorb the experiences of the past 21 years and set out new goals. The assumption made was that everyone would wish to see Wooden Spoon continue to flourish and grow. Therefore, we set about producing a plan based upon sustained growth that would enable Spoon to disperse more funds to disadvantaged children and young people. I must say right up front that Spoon is all about working in partnership with others and having fun

Clifford Chance is pleased to support
Wooden Spoon.

www.cliffordchance.com

CLIFFORD

CHANCE

MORE POWERFUL LEGAL SOLUTIONS

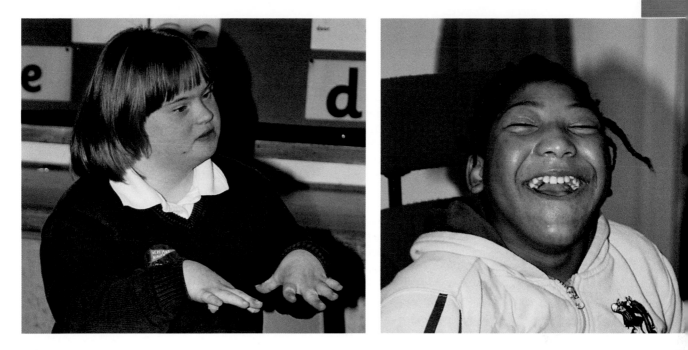

ABOVE AND ABOVE RIGHT Children from Woodlands School, Leatherhead, Surrey, at a recent visit by Wooden Spoon and staff from TNT, who have supported so many Spoon projects.

BELOW TNT staff visit children supported by Disability Challengers in Guildford, who provide specialist play facilities for disabled children.

along the way. While we are deadly serious about our work, our 'fun-raising' mantra will come through loud and clear at all our events!

There are four guiding principles of a financial nature that set Wooden Spoon apart from many organisations. They are:

1. Money raised in a region is spent in that region: what we call 'local funds for local projects'.

2. Money raised in a region is doubled by Wooden Spoon's national fund-raising initiatives.

3. Administration costs are very closely monitored and maintained to levels of below ten per cent achieved throughout the past decade.

4. High standards in our codes of practice are always sought.

The four principles applied together create a charity of national significance with local impact, accountability and financial credibility. All of this is made possible thanks to a very special group of people –

our regional volunteers. Some 400 men and women throughout the UK and Ireland organise fund-raising events for Spoon within their local communities. This unpaid workforce is the backbone of the charity and a key to our successful development. The character as well as the success of Spoon is grounded in their many hours of selfless hard work – we are lucky and always grateful to have them!

As strange as it may seem, Wooden Spoon and the world of rugby have grown closer over the past year. Our patrons – the Home Unions – are working more closely with us, creating opportunities for Spoon to raise funds, giving us promotional opportunities and taking an active interest in our work. For example, since England's victory in the World Cup, the RFU has generously been fund-raising and promoting our work while circulating the country with the Sweet Chariot Tour.

Worcester Rugby Club celebrated promotion to the Premiership this year in great style by donating all gate receipts from their pre-season friendly against Leinster to Wooden Spoon. Such generosity, for which we are truly grateful, will enable us to fund a new project in the Worcester area – and generosity of this kind is not uncommon in rugby circles and among Spoon supporters. Whether you are chairman of

BELOW Wooden Spoon CEO Geoff Morris receives a cheque for £70,000 from RFU president Robert Horner, representing a pound on each seat sold at the England v New Zealand Barbarians game in December 2003.

London Welsh and a life member of Spoon, or cheering on Tigers from the stands and quietly paying your annual subscription, or reading this book in the comfort of the Wooden Spoon corner at Newcastle Falcons – you are all greatly appreciated.

We are proud to be working with The School for Hard Knocks for a third consecutive year. The school brings together youngsters who have never been introduced to the game of rugby, with players of international standing acting as their coaches. This formula has seen the Hard Knocks team train with the world famous Barbarians, the England Sevens squad and eventually compete in the National Schools Sevens in their own right.

At the other end of the age spectrum, Spoon has joined forces with the indomitable Anti-Assassins to form the SpoonAAs. The famous 53-year-old Anti-Assassins Rugby Club (A-As) will help us to promote our charitable work. The A-As' membership includes over 100 internationals and two past presidents of the RFU, as well as Malcolm Phillips, the current president. Bill Beaumont, the next Lions manager is also a member. John Spencer, the chairman of Club England, is the A-A president.

In future, the rugby team 'SpoonAAs' will play a mixture of traditional fixtures and special anniversary matches, and the fixtures against Oxford and Cambridge Universities will be resurrected. Added to these games will be some high-profile events such as the Hong Kong Tens, the Dubai Sevens and the Caribbean Sevens.

Each fixture will raise money for disabled and disadvantaged children and help to raise the profile of Wooden Spoon. The association will increase Spoon membership and so aid our charitable work. Rugby people, players, past players and administrators can thus harmonise their love of the game and help disadvantaged younger people too. With the association, this formidable membership will create a national and international community embracing rugby people in many different countries.

Last year saw Spoon intervene to help the National Schools Sevens to find a sponsor to keep the world's largest rugby tournament alive. Such has been the interest in our work from participating schools that the sevens will become a focal point for new fund-raising for the charity. This is an exciting prospect for us. Every organisation seeks to inject new enthusiasm and fresh ideas, and where better for Spoon to look than among the thousands of participants in this famous event?

Spoon has created its own virtual rugby team – without doubt world-beaters with a social consciousness to match. I am referring to the Wooden Spoon First XV, a growing squad of loyal and committed corporate supporters. Their combined efforts in cash and in kind will contribute over £750,000 to our work this year!

People's generosity never ceases to amaze me – at a recent Spoon golf day, four members of the local club who were patiently following the tails of our event, enquired 'What is this Wooden Spoon, then?' Upon hearing the reply, they promptly agreed a £100 wager for the remainder of their round and donated the proceeds to Spoon in the bar afterwards! There are hundreds of similar stories of generosity that provide us with the funding to do our work – Thank you.

Once again, Mr Robertson has pulled out all the stops to produce a great read – a book that everyone at Spoon is really proud to call our own. I must take this opportunity to warmly thank Ian for his years of support to Wooden Spoon. Ian has produced this annual for 17 years, raising funds and the profile of the charity's work in the process. Without his effort, supported by Lennard Associates and Queen Anne Press and the generosity of sponsors Powergen and Travis Perkins, we would not be able to make the claim of being 'the only charity in the UK with a hardback annual'. In quiet moments, I think fondly of Ian bobbing aimlessly on that fictitious rowing machine when Martin Johnson bursts into the gym. You all know how the story ends …

Geoff Morris
Chief Executive
Wooden Spoon

If you are not a member and would like to join Wooden Spoon, please take a look at our website www.woodenspoon.com for details or telephone 01276 410180.

REACH
FOR THE BEST

It's rare to find a recruitment consultancy who tackle personnel requirements with such tenacity and unfailing dedication. An unrivalled approach that has enabled Pertemps to remain unchallenged at the top of the league as the UK's leading independent recruitment consultancy.

As market leaders, we have developed our reputation not just by "filling positions" but by adding value to our client portfolio, a philosophy which is reflected in the diverse range of leading blue-chip companies that currently utilise our services.

Operating in three service divisions: commercial and professional, industrial and driving and technical and executive, our fully integrated service ensures that we are able to deliver quality personnel with the right skills, in the right place at the right time.

So, if you are seeking to win the competition for business, make sure that you retain the competition for talent by choosing Jobs@Pertemps, Britain's most successful independent recruitment consultancy.

COMMENT
& FEATURES

What Now for Martin Johnson?

by MARTIN JOHNSON of *The Daily Telegraph*

'He could, of course, end up in the television analyst's booth, probably making his co-commentators smile when obliged to "tut tut" at some bout of fisticuffs among the forwards.'

He certainly bears the scars of battle. If he got captured by cannibals, the ears would be first onto the plate – served up with a nice helping of cheese sauce – and the face looks as though it might have been involved in a recent collision with an Eddie Stobart truck. Cue hospital spokesman. 'I'm pleased to say that Martin Johnson spent a comfortable night, but sadly there was nothing we could do to save the lorry.'

So how much longer for Jonno? England is now the past, the buzz of holding the World Cup making him realise that only anticlimax awaited inside a white shirt, and Leicester are keeping a seat warm for him somewhere at Welford Road when he feels he can no longer offer the Tigers what he once used to. Johnson behind a desk in a suit is a picture that's hard to conjure up, even though that's how he started his professional life, as a bank teller in Market Harborough. Needless to say, the branch never got robbed.

Johnson is a far more eloquent man in private than in a public press conference, so maybe the after-dinner circuit awaits. His Leicester chief executive Peter Wheeler is testimony to the fact that it's not only the backs who have the intelligence and wit to entertain the brandy-and-cigar audiences up and down the country. Wheeler's own experiences in an England shirt, and, like Johnson, as captain of his country, provide a rich fund of stories and anecdotes, and none goes down better than the match against Australia at Twickenham in 1979 – immortalised forever as the Erica Roe game.

Ms Roe, whose frontage would have caused her to spill over from Page 3 to Page 4 in *The Sun*, made her famous entry at half-time, and Billy Beaumont's stirring speech to the troops (remember when the players only had five minutes to catch their breath and suck an orange) disintegrated when scrum half Steve Smith piped up: 'Eh, Bill. Some bird's just run on with your bum on her chest.'

Johnson, of course, is mainly a product of the professional era, where such stories hardly ever intrude on what is now a serious business. However, he still spans the old amateur era as well, and there will be no shortage of stories to tell. Like so many players of his age, he has memories of the old amateur game, when the post-match ritual was not so much having half a shandy in the sponsor's lounge as downing 20 pints in the members' bar, during which some prop forward would break wind to the accompaniment of a lighted match.

LEFT World champion captain. Martin Johnson on the rampage during the final of Rugby World Cup 2003 at Sydney's Telstra Stadium.

RIGHT Taking part in full and frank discussions with New Zealand referee Paul Honiss – England v France, Twickenham, 2003.

He was a shy lad when he first came to Leicester, and his first bar duty involved an international giving him a massive beer order, and Johnson not knowing what to charge him. The orderer dumped a massive pile of change onto the bar, and when Jonno came to scoop it up, he realised that it was all in Spanish pesetas.

Johnson's career as one of the world's most feared and admired No. 4s made him a cross between Willie John McBride and Colin Meads. McBride's players would have followed him anywhere, and probably only McBride's players would have followed him down a dark alley in the knowledge that Meads was at the end of it. 'Not much grass is there?' said McBride to Meads as he led out the Lions against the All Blacks on a typical New Zealand mudheap. To which Meads growled, without so much as glancing sideways at his opposite number, 'We've not come here to graze.'

It is a moot point as to whether Johnson would make a good job of coaching, or whether Leicester will employ him in some other capacity. He is as iconic a figure as Dean Richards was, although Richards's demise as head coach there does suggest that sentiment – in modern day rugby at any rate – is no longer a bottomless commodity.

Like Richards, Johnson was idolised all the more for being a man entirely without ego. He constantly meets people who are surprised that he comes into a pub with his wife and sits quietly with a smallish drink, rather than coming in a bit like a Western movie desperado – the guy in the Stetson that causes the piano player to come to an abrupt halt.

However, Johnson knows better than anyone what it's like to be pigeon-holed, having done a few things on a rugby field that he's not especially proud of. The man dubbed 'Neanderthal' by one journalist after treading on John Leslie's throat during an England v Scotland match got a bit upset by that one, as the video later proved it to be a complete accident. Nevertheless, ever mindful that it didn't hurt England for him to have a reputation for – how can we put it – being able to look after himself, Johnson confessed with a smile that if Leslie hadn't accidentally rolled out of a ruck to get in the way of his left foot, he was going to give him a 'shoe-ing' with his right.

Johnson will, like many others before him, miss the adrenalin rush that comes with playing rugby at the highest level, and confesses to dreading the absence of that Saturday afternoon (or, nowadays, Sunday evening – depending on the Sky TV schedules) buzz just before kick-off time. He and Austin Healey, he revealed recently, had decided to become bank robbers (an interesting twist for someone who once used to work in one) to recapture the adrenalin, but Johnson then thought better of it when conjuring up an image of the motormouthed Healey calling a press conference to tell the police exactly how they'd done it.

He could, of course, end up in the television analyst's booth, probably making his co-commentators smile when obliged to 'tut tut' at some bout of fisticuffs among the forwards. It was the same for David Gower when he retired from cricket and found himself in the Sky box taking some hapless left-hander to task for an airy-fairy waft outside the off stump.

The leadership qualities that have made Johnson the only player to captain the Lions twice were not immediately apparent when he took over the England job, but one reason his team-mates looked up to him (apart from the obvious reason of being 6ft 7ins) is the fact that he doesn't speak very often. 'I am,' he once said, 'no Winston Churchill,' but the point about Johnson is that when he does open his mouth – one or two referees would say far too often – he makes it count.

He will remain in rugby, most probably in a capacity in which his motivational qualities are harnessed to the best effect. And when he joins the after-dinner speaking circuit, his audiences might be surprised at how gentle and intelligent his delivery is. The image of Johnson I retain above all from England's victory in the World Cup is not the one in which he's holding the Webb Ellis trophy aloft but in the lobby of a Sydney hotel one night, two days before a big game. The hotel had been more or less taken over by a party of Leicester supporters, and Johnson was signing shirts, books, beer mats, foreheads, you name it, for the thick end of two hours. And he never once failed to give the impression that there was nothing he'd rather have been doing with his evening. As you might gather from a man with Desperate Dan stubble who also advertised Bic razors, there are two sides to Martin Johnson – and both of them mark him out as the most singular of sportsmen.

Fortunam Velut Tunicam ...

by PAUL STEPHENS

'... something must be done; or the Premiership sides will look like Arsenal, dominated perhaps not by Frenchmen but by mercenaries from the southern hemisphere.'

The orgy of congratulation, adulation and back-slapping after England's World Cup triumph in Australia, with the gongs raining down like hailstones on all those who took part, had to end sometime; though the manner of its ending was not what Sir Clive Woodward would have wanted, with an unconvincing showing in the Six Nations Championship, followed by a disastrous summer tour to the southern hemisphere. What a reality check!

Hindsight being infinitely more reliable than forecasting, it is still instructive to enquire how England are preparing for the future. One pointer could be gained from the Under 21 World Championship, which was held in Scotland last June. I was fortunate to be at Galashiels for the opening match between England and the eventual winners, New Zealand. I say match, though the way the impressively mature and powerful junior All Blacks despatched some of England's finest youngsters 42-13, it was more of a mismatch. In another two or three years, when these Kiwis have grown up, I know who my money will be on when they face European opposition. Are the academies in England turning out young players with the potential to become fully fledged internationals? On the evidence of what I saw at Netherdale in the Scottish Borders, the answer is a resounding no.

Not that this has deterred those who delight in repeating the mantra about the game in England being in such rude health. Try telling this to the good folk of Wakefield, West Hartlepool or Orrell, and you can expect pretty short shrift; as you can from the former members of Headingley and Roundhay, very few of whom have transferred their allegiance to the Leeds Tykes, after a merger of the two clubs led to the formation of the professional outfit. The icy blast of enduring discomfort, not to say disenchantment, with rugby's new order is not confined exclusively to clubs in the north. Where are Richmond and London Scottish now? There will be other casualties, no doubt, as clubs continue to spend above their means in the vain hope that it will guarantee success, though one only has to look at little Otley in leafy Wharfedale to see how it is possible to play attractive, winning rugby within the confines of a very tight budget.

Whatever our concerns for the future of the clubs in the divisions immediately below the Zurich Premiership and those who find themselves in straitened circumstances, four paramount issues face the game. These are the almost inhuman demands being asked of the senior players, who play far more rugby than is good for them; franchising; the growing number of foreign nationals plying their trade with the leading English clubs (many of these players are denying younger, England-qualified players invaluable top-level experience); and last, though by no means least, the way the Premiership conducts itself, with an apparent disregard for its own regulations.

LEFT Mike Harrison, the England captain, scores a try against Australia in Sydney during the 1987 World Cup. Harrison, who spent his entire career with Wakefield, is mortified that the College Grove club has folded.

BELOW A rare moment in the limelight for once-great Orrell, who celebrate victory in the Powergen Shield final after they beat Exeter at Twickenham in April 2003. Will they ever be mighty again now that owner Dave Whelan has decided not to fund them as a professional club? Coach Ross Reynolds (standing, fourth from right) has jumped ship to coach Rotherham in an attempt to help them return to the Premiership.

Acres of space have already been devoted to the undesirability of round-the-calendar rugby, and I have no wish to give the subject a further airing, except to say that England's chances of further international achievement will inevitably be weakened unless finding a solution to the absurd scheduling of never-ending rugby is given a higher priority.

The warning signs of the dangers of franchising – or to put it in proper context, buy-outs or the acquisition of clubs by wealthy businessmen who have no connection with rugby in England and no feel for its culture – was raised recently in an attempt by one of South Africa's richest entrepreneurs, Johann Rupert. This dangerous dreamer's commercial interests include Dunhill and Cartier. He first tried to buy a National One club and, once rebuffed, then wanted to pour money into London Tribe, which would be a satellite South African side, with Premiership aspirations and all that goes with them. The consequences should Rupert succeed would have far-reaching implications. If Rupert could do it, why not some sharp-suited impresario from New Zealand, or Argentina, or Australia? If it didn't work, as it patently did not for Frank Warren at Bedford and Ashley Levett at Richmond, the freebooters could ride off into the sunset, leaving behind them a trail of debt and unfulfilled ambitions.

Sure, in soccer there has been the controversial relocation of Wimbledon to Milton Keynes, which was only legitimised after much soul-searching, not to mention widespread displeasure, among the fans in southwest London. But do we want this for rugby? I think it unlikely, if only because of the dangers of leading the game not towards the promised land but into a quagmire of uncertainty and mistrust. Club rugby has been through enough transformations in one decade thank you; and not all have proved beneficial.

Because of an appreciable increase in Premiership attendances, there is an unrestrained assumption that all is well with the club game, if not with England. This piece of rapturous tosh takes no account of the change that has done English rugby the most far-reaching disservice, which is the cascade of overseas players securing their employment in the Premiership. While we marvel at Arsenal's season of wonder during which the Gunners scored more than 100 goals, let us remember that only four were claimed by England-qualified players. In cricket, when Derbyshire revealed their squad for the summer, seven of the first nine on the list were not qualified to play for England.

As things stand, the Rugby Football Union and England Rugby Ltd (ERL) – the latter being responsible for overseeing the Premiership – appear hypnotised by the ramifications of the Kolpak Agreement, which is an important component of European employment law. This came into force

LEFT Naka Drotske, one of a growing number of South Africans earning their corn in the Premiership. The London Irish hooker offloads before receiving the attention of Newcastle's Dave Walder.

BELOW A familiar sight in today's Premiership. Northampton's rebuilt Franklin's Gardens stadium has few empty seats as attendances continue their upward spiral.

after Maros Kolpak, a Slovakian handball player, managed to get the European Court of Justice to rule him eligible to play for Germany without being classed as a foreigner, because his country has an associate arrangement with the EU. Similarly, the Cotonou Agreement gives workers from African countries and the Caribbean identical rights, because of a trade affiliation with the EU. Australia and New Zealand are soon to sign similar accords, which will push the floodgates open even wider.

If we are to avoid a scenario in which the greater percentage of players in the Premiership are foreigners – although they may have a perfectly legitimate right to work in the UK – there must be a commitment towards restricting to two or three the number of players not qualified to play for England who are permitted in a match-day squad. Believing that the clubs would regulate such a concord voluntarily is like expecting the police to dismantle all the roadside speed cameras, so the way forward is for the RFU to centrally contract all England-qualified players, in order to have complete control over who can and cannot play. Does it seem too radical? Yes. Is it impossible? Not if there is sufficient will among those who understand the extent of the problem and the likely consequences if it is not confronted. If the RFU and England Rugby Ltd are to stay signed up to the understanding that the top of the pyramid must remain occupied by England and the needs of the national team come first, something must be done; or the Premiership sides will look like Arsenal, dominated perhaps not by Frenchmen but by mercenaries from the southern hemisphere.

If the alarm bells aren't ringing loudly over this conundrum, then the administrators of the game in England will have only themselves to blame if the Premiership becomes a league of nations. Equally, there will be a catastrophic lack of trust unless the Premiership pays due and consistent regard to its own regulations. Among these is the insistence that all Premiership clubs must have a stadium which can accommodate a minimum of 8,200 spectators. A promoted club, if its ground doesn't meet this criterion, has two choices: either to increase the capacity of its facility or to move to a ground which does satisfy the regulation. Either way, these arrangements have to be in place by 31 March of the year in which a club is promoted. Thus Worcester were affected as they won last season's National One by a distance.

RIGHT The Minister for Sport, the Rt Hon Richard Caborn MP, addressing a Twickenham audience in 2003, at the launch of Rugby – Making an Impact. Caborn has had plenty to say on the way Worcester's promotion has been handled by England Rugby Ltd. With his department bolstering the RFU's finances to the tune of £3.1 million each year, Caborn believes that the way it was managed was not in the best interests of the game; and there should be more clarity about promotion and relegation.

Two years ago it was Rotherham who came up against this regulation. Their cramped Clifton Lane ground was too small, so they agreed to share with the town's football club at Millmoor, which has a capacity exceeding 9,000. However, they were denied promotion, because the lease had not been signed before the March cut-off point. This meant a reprieve for bottom-placed Leeds, and acute disappointment, if not embarrassment, for Rotherham. Mike Yarlett, the South Yorkshire club's owner, said: 'We missed out on promotion, and had to accept our failure on technical grounds; and we did so with good grace. All clubs are aware of the entry regulations, but England Rugby seems to ignore them.'

Rotherham's current chagrin stems from the realisation that Worcester did not have their planning consent in place before 31 March. Indeed their application to extend a stand at Sixways was not received by Wychavon District Council until 8 April, and consent was not granted until 9 May. Even then the local authority, police and those responsible for safety, mindful of the dangers of larger crowds being decanted on to the narrow road which services Worcester's ground, had not given their permission for any enlargement.

Francis Baron, chief executive of ERL, in acknowledging this, said: 'There was no limitation on Worcester's capacity, but the planning for this is due to expire in December and it was necessary to have consent in place for the full season. So the board of England Rugby Ltd used their discretion, just as they had in Rotherham's case when they didn't have primacy of tenure at Millmoor. We are satisfied entirely that our processes are robust and that we have behaved properly.'

It is the element of discretion and obfuscation which will give rise to some concerns, not only at Rotherham, who feel very hard done to, but also with the Minister for Sport, Richard Caborn. 'When I spoke to England Rugby Ltd,' said Caborn, 'they declared that it wasn't possible to answer my questions, because the matter was in the hands of their solicitors.

'As I see it, and you will appreciate that it is very difficult for a minister to get involved – even though my department funds the RFU to the extent of £3.1 million a year towards the development of rugby – so I have to be even-handed. But there has been a bias here which is not in the best interests of the game. It is an unsatisfactory situation, for there appears to have been a major difference of interpretation. England Rugby Ltd have failed to deal with this, and in my view there must be much more transparency and clarity about promotion and relegation.'

While there is much to applaud about the Premiership, there is no reason for complacency, and those of that mind would do well to remember the words of Apuleius: *Fortunam velut tunicam, magis concinnam proba, quam longam.* Judge your fortune as you judge a coat; look not at the size of it, but see that it fits.

The Premiership coat fits reasonably well and is far from threadbare, but it could do with a trip to the dry cleaners.

What People Want
the 2005 Lions to New Zealand

by **MICK CLEARY**

'People cherish the Lions not because of tribal roots but because of a love of sport in its purest essence. The Lions constitute a unique concept.'

I t's not a precise science. And that's even if you avoid the five pints of old wallop and three-hour taproom consultation in the local pub. Selection for the British and Irish Lions is an ever-changing process. The names change and the context shifts. That's what makes the exercise such fun. That's what makes the whole operation so rich in possibilities. And the endless game of permutations tells you why the Lions are such an enduring entity.

It was once argued that the dawn of the professional era would bring instant darkness for the Lions. Too much rugby. Too many competing interests. Too much staked on the Rugby World Cup. Individual countries would be committed to their own agendas, driven to

ABOVE 'Some 20,000 British and Irish fans materialised in Australia, drawn from far-flung parts ...' Jason Robinson runs towards a red corner to score the opening try for the Lions in the first Test v Australia at Brisbane 2001.

protecting and developing their own money-spinning ventures. And what national coach would want to see his players disappear for a whole summer just to trade titbits with players from rival countries?

So much for the theory. Logic disappeared up its own backside. The triumph of the Lions concept is a triumph for consumerism. The punters voted with their feet and their wallets for what they liked best. It gladdens the heart to see the ordinary bloke and woman win the day. It doesn't happen too

often. We don't always take too kindly to being told what to do and what to like, as was shown with the great CAMRA uprising of the late 1970s and early 1980s. (The generation weaned on Bacardi Breezers and tequila shots may wish to switch off at this point.) The Campaign for Real Ale overthrew the combined interests of the big brewers who were intent on forcing gassy urine down our throats camouflaged as beer.

Well, the Campaign for Real Rugby has found its niche with the Lions. The 2001 tour to Australia was a landmark trip. The series may have been lost, but the status of every future Lions tour was guaranteed. Some 20,000 British and Irish fans materialised in Australia, drawn from far-flung parts – from Limerick and Llanelli to expat communities in Singapore and Sydney. It was a mass outburst of support, not just for the native isles but, to my mind, for an endangered sporting species.

People cherish the Lions not because of tribal roots but because of a love of sport in its purest essence. The Lions constitute a unique concept. No other sporting entity embraces the diverse frontiers of the four home countries. The players are thrown together and they have to get on with it. The supporters adopt a similar outlook.

One of the gripes levelled by the put-upon 2001 Lions, a fractious party at times, was that certain practices didn't match up to the professional standards of certain individual countries. While not excusing sloppiness or neglect in back-up areas such as nutrition and rehabilitation, there was an easy counter to that line of argument – how can it compare? The Lions have nowhere near the same time together, the same sense of familiarity and ease of communication. They haven't spent weeks and weeks through the season, year after year, drilling themselves senseless on defence. They can't recite codes of line-out calls as if they were parrots with studs on. They don't have instant recall of the miss-two move denoting a cut-out sequence involving the blind-side wing. And they are all the better for that. The onus shifts far more on to the players to sort it all out for themselves. That is what coaches have to understand with the Lions. You don't have the same time and access. You have to do it differently.

That is where the appeal and charm and magic lies – for players as well as for spectators. It's time for coaches to buy into that. One of the most revealing statements I've come across in the past

12 months came from All Black and former Northampton coach Wayne Smith. In the aftermath of New Zealand's thumping win in the first Test over England, Smith revealed that the back line had kept it simple because they hadn't had much time together. Looked like a formula they should stick with as Joe Rokocoko and his mates ripped England to shreds. Give players opportunity and they rarely let you down.

So power to the players. And power to the people. They have already signed up in their thousands for the six-week trek round New Zealand. There is not a bed to be had this side of Invercargill. As ever, the poor old punter is being made to pay through the back pocket for hotel rooms, and with limited capacity in New Zealand stadiums the only way he can guarantee a match ticket is to book with an official travel operator. Let's hope that the background is not too corporate. The beauty of the 2001 Lions tour to Australia as well as the World Cup three years later was that the rank and file took over the terraces and stands. They didn't give a tinker's cuss about being properly suited and booted. They gave it a lash, and the atmosphere was both colourful and raucous.

There is one other simple truth about the Lions that needs to be highlighted. We only see them once every four years. And we are all much the better for that. Less is more – a mantra that runs counter to every single philosophy that seems to have governed rugby in the past decade. You can't draw breath before some union or commercial concern is proposing another match, another competition, another tour. The fans have had enough, so too the players, although they will never bleat much, as their bank balances are being bolstered by the excessive schedule.

The Lions, God bless 'em, only want to do business once in a while. Their opening hours are restricted also to overseas tours. That too adds to their exoticism and rarity value. There is a break with that tradition this time around with a revenue-raising match planned prior to departure. Argentina have been lined up as likely opponents for the Lions, who feel obliged to raise monies in order to meet their desired budgetary aim of compensating clubs for player release, putting a few bob in the coffers of each union and also bringing together the biggest-ever squad of players and coaches for the 11-match trip.

It's a professional game and the need for cash is evident. I wonder, though, if a dangerous precedent has not been set by staging the fund-raiser. How long before there is a call for a mini-Lions tour, to France perhaps or to play against some trumped-up World XV for some cause or other? I know that

LEFT Embracing frontiers. Dafydd James of Wales, supported by Keith Wood of Ireland and England's Martin Johnson – second Test v Australia, Melbourne 2001.

BELOW World Cup-winning coach Sir Clive Woodward has charge of the Lions for the 2005 trip to New Zealand.

there have been one or two exceptions to the rule in the past that the Lions only ever congregate overseas, but once that convention is broken, then all manner of possibilities are opened up. Tread carefully, for you tread on our dreams.

What then of this Lions vintage? The tour has been trimmed to the bare minimum. Ten matches were originally scheduled, although the push for an eleventh came from the Lions management. They realised that potentially the most corrosive element in any Lions party centres around those not required for Test duty. No player of any standard has ambitions only to hold a tackle bag. Extend that argument all the way up to the most elite level, and you can appreciate just what sort of discontent might fester.

ABOVE Brian O'Driscoll's elusive centre partner Gordon D'Arcy attempts to evade Gareth Thomas, a member of Wales's eye-catching back three.

RIGHT Iestyn Harris is confronted by Lions contenders Tom Smith, Gordon Bulloch and Simon Taylor of Scotland.

It's a statement of the blindingly obvious that a sizeable chunk of a touring party will not be involved in Test action. However, they have to be made to feel involved, to feel wanted and worthwhile. Even big boys need comforting. Hence Clive Woodward's laudable decision to take two distinct coaching teams with him. The three-man groups will have responsibility for a team a week – the dirt-trackers and the Saturday team. They will have time to prepare both themselves and the men that end up in that particular combination. So, even if a player realises pretty early on that his role in this Lions life is to be the understudy to, say, Jonny Wilkinson, then at least he knows that he will have a full and active role to play in trying to preserve an unbeaten record for the midweek side against the New Zealand provinces.

That didn't happen in the 2001 Lions. And it hasn't happened in many Lions squads before that. The added game – the eleventh fixture – is designed to take place between the second and third Tests, the week when those on the fringes are at their lowest ebb. Good decision.

The Lions captain is a key figure in any party. With such a big group – 44 players and 26 back-up staff – this time around, he assumes even more importance. He has to set the tone, to strike the right balance between work and play, and to ensure that the management team live up to its stated aim of the party being a broad church.

There are two main contenders in the frame at the time of writing – England's Lawrence Dallaglio and Ireland's Brian O'Driscoll. My preference would be for Dallaglio. He conducted himself wonderfully well in tough times during England's trip to New Zealand and Australia. He managed to play well even in adversity and is a fully paid-up member of the live-life-to-the-full club. Work hard and play hard is not the worst motto for the 2005 Lions.

As for the rest of the party, there are no end of permutations to offer. The fears that England would swamp selection no longer look so likely to come to pass after the summer lapses. The Celts will make their mark through double acts such as O'Driscoll and Gordon D'Arcy in midfield and Malcolm O'Kelly and Paul O'Connell in the second row with Donncha O'Callaghan thrown in for good measure. Scotland, for all their limp showing in last year's Six Nations, can offer a clutch of Test contenders in prop Tom Smith, hooker Gordon Bulloch, lock Scott Murray and No. 8 Simon Taylor – albeit with fingers crossed that Taylor makes a recovery from injury. And Wales? Intriguing possibilities there, the most tantalising of which is that Rob Howley will contest his third Lions tour even though he has retired from international rugby. Gareth Cooper is no slouch at scrum half either, while Wales's back three – Gareth Thomas, Rhys Williams and Shane Williams – were the pick of last season's championship. Watch out, too, for utility forward Michael Owen, as talented a ball player as his soccer namesake.

There are plenty of names to go into the hat. The Lions are in good order.

Lawrence Dallaglio
A Year to Remember

by STEPHEN JONES

'The men you always want on your side are those who can deliver something special, even when things are not going their way. We call them winners – and Dallaglio has always had that aura about him.'

Picture the scene – a coffee kiosk in the transit lounge at Singapore airport, and England's finest are jet-lagged and drained of energy after the ill-fated 2004 summer tour of New Zealand and Australia. The end of what has often seemed like an endless season is finally in sight, and touchdown at Heathrow in 14 hours will bring welcome and much-needed respite for weary, battered bodies. The gentlemen of the rugby press have had a hard trip of it.

However, there's someone out of place. Lawrence Dallaglio simply doesn't do the dishevelled hack very well, even though having foot-slogged through the full, unexpurgated horror of Dunedin, Auckland and Brisbane at the end of a hugely punishing two-year season he has more right than the rest of us to look completely wrecked.

But for the captain of England, the tour is not yet over. The departing crew, individually, want their pictures taken with him, so, with unflinching good humour, Dallaglio smiles for the camera as ham-fisted journos get the chance to play David Bailey. Then, just as he sits down to sip his latte, the autograph hunters arrive. He does the signature session without batting an eyelid. When the last of his admirers have gone, he says, 'It's fine, especially as in a few years' time they won't know me from Adam'.

I disagree. In the past year Dallaglio, 32, has become a giant of the modern game, acquiring a status which rivals even that of Martin Johnson, who succeeded him as England captain when a tabloid sting forced him to relinquish the role in 1999. What is more, since regaining the captaincy after Johnson's retirement, the Wasps No. 8 has earned giant status despite having to lead an England side which, minus the grit and nous of Johnson and Neil Back and deprived of Jonny Wilkinson's match-winning properties, plummeted from its World Cup peak in the intervening seven months.

England's reputation would have fallen a lot further without Dallaglio to stop the slide, as England's World Cup-

RIGHT Lawrence Dallaglio sets off on a trademark charge with the old firm of Neil Back and Richard Hill in support – 2003 World Cup final, Sydney.

winning coach, Sir Clive Woodward, acknowledged when he paid tribute to his skipper's 'outstanding' contribution following the battering meted out to the world champions on their return to the southern hemisphere in June.

However, the true measure of Dallaglio, the leader and the player, can only be appreciated from a clear analysis of what he has achieved for both his country and his club over the past year. But first, we need to delve back further. Irked at having been dropped by Woodward for low work rate against New Zealand in the autumn of 2002, despite making 19 tackles in the match, Dallaglio moved into overdrive for the rest of the pre-World Cup season. Restored to the England side for the Six Nations, he scored a try in the Grand Slam triumph over Ireland in Dublin, and then led Wasps to the English championship, his side thrashing Gloucester in the Zurich Premiership final, having already beaten Bath in the Parker Pen Challenge Cup final.

It was no mean preamble to the short tour Down Under in June 2003, when England set out their World Cup stall by beating New Zealand and Australia on consecutive weekends. For Dallaglio, who is aware of the game's great traditions, the gratuitous disrespect shown by the New Zealand media and public for England's credentials when they arrived in Wellington was all the motivation he needed. It was his first trip to New Zealand, and he was determined to make his mark. Stripping candy from a baby was the phrase that came to mind as the 6ft 4ins, 17st 4lbs Londoner ripped ball off All Black forwards at will, and the power and savvy he showed at close quarters played a key part in a famous England victory (15-13), despite the No. 8 being sin-binned in the second half.

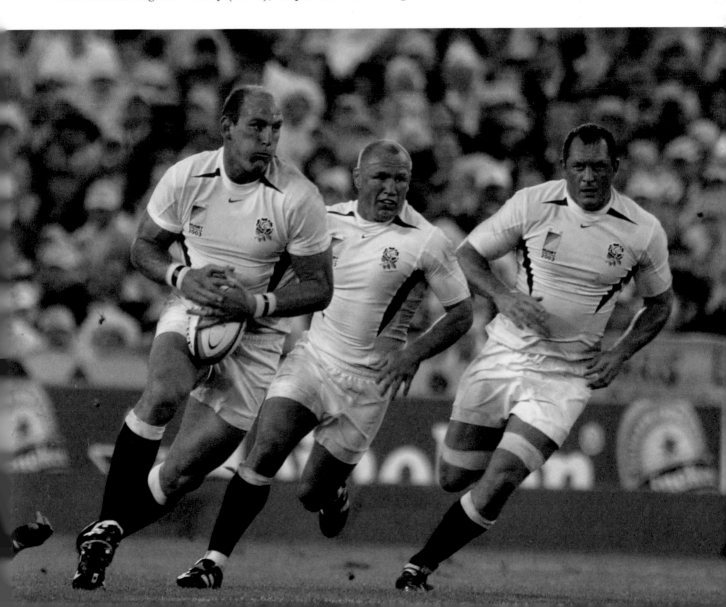

Seven days later in Melbourne, Dallaglio was equally conspicuous in England's three-tries-to-one trouncing of the Wallabies (25-14), a display which, with the benefit of hindsight, many view as the high performance point on England's road to becoming world champions. This first victory on Australian soil was, without doubt, a great display, but for me it was surpassed by the sheer guts and enterprise England showed in beating Australia in the 2003 World Cup final five months later.

No one encapsulated England's unyielding competitive spirit in the 2003 World Cup more than Dallaglio. Nothing appeals to the Antipodean psyche more than a never-say-die fighter – so much so that they have had the neck to appropriate it as their very own quality, as in 'he's a true Aussie battler'. In Dallaglio they met an English battler who was every inch their match.

Having already peaked three times in the season before the World Cup – England's Grand Slam, Wasps' championship and England's Anzac tour double – Dallaglio was then asked to play every minute of England's seven matches during the tournament. He was the only player to do so. If in the

HAVE

PROUD SPONSORS OF

early pool matches against Georgia, South Africa and Samoa, Dallaglio looked a little stale, he was not alone. England were not at their best – hardly surprising given that the likes of Dallaglio had only three weeks off between the end of one season and reporting for England's World Cup training camp. Effectively one season had merged with the other. Therefore, it was understandable that when Woodward singled out Dallaglio for being below his best at a press conference prior to the Brisbane quarter-final against Wales, he was stunned. Whether Woodward deliberately goaded Dallaglio, or whether he inadvertently named just one player, is a moot point. The known quantity was that, of all his players, Woodward understood that no one would thrive on overcoming adversity more than Dallaglio.

His character has been built on it since his world was torn apart as a teenager by the death of his sister, Francesca, in the *Marchioness* river-boat disaster. Rugby helped him to cope with the grief, as well as to develop an unshakeable self-belief and determination to complement his athletic prowess. It has carried him through the tabloid-inspired social drug use 'confessions' which saw him resign the England captaincy, and helped him to recover from a career-threatening knee ligament injury after the 2001 Lions tour.

The men you always want on your side are those who can deliver something special, even when

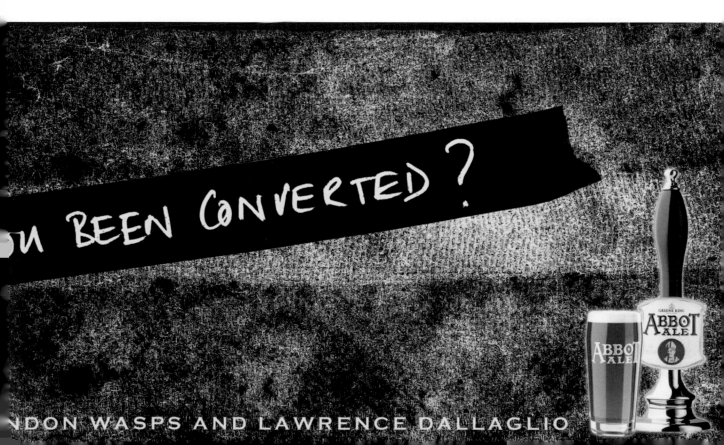

When it came to delivering in the biggest game in England's history, Dallaglio stepped up. Australia held all the aces going into the final – home advantage, an extra day's rest, and an all-southern hemisphere officiating team dedicated to upholding Super 12 interpretations of the laws, including neutering England's clear scrummaging superiority. All the aces, perhaps, but Dallaglio held the trump card. Jeremy Guscott, a close friend of Dallaglio, believes that his competitive edge is so keen that he is unwilling to let even his best mates get one up on him. As Guscott put it, 'Tell him you are going to Tenerife and he'll be going to Elevenerife.'

The Dallaglio edge was sharp enough to mortally wound the Wallabies. In a final dominated by sledgehammer defences, Dallaglio's arcing break past Stirling Mortlock typified what winners are made of. It unlocked the Aussie gate, and his precision pass out of the tackle to Jonny Wilkinson set up Jason Robinson's try and paved the way to a 20-17 victory.

Although Woodward cogitated for a few weeks after Johnson's retirement over his successor, Dallaglio was the only player with the credentials to take over the mantle. And, despite a wretched season on the scoreboard in the Six Nations and on the summer tour, it has proved conclusively to be the right choice. On the pitch he has provided the muscle in a recast back row, showing phenomenal reserves of stamina and determination. Even the curmudgeonly New Zealanders showed respect when in the second Test at Eden Park he emerged from the bowels of the second row – where he had gone after the ludicrous decision to send off Simon Shaw ten minutes into the match – to haul down the speedy Nick Evans from a fingertip grip to save a try.

Dallaglio has proved that he is no fair-weather leader, and off the pitch he has been equally stalwart. He has shown himself to be articulate and honest in assessing England's shortcomings in what has been a brutal rebuilding period since becoming world champions. With the Six Nations losses to Ireland and France followed by the drubbings inflicted by New Zealand and Australia, England finished the season with five defeats from their last six games. Dallaglio's answer to why it all went so badly wrong? Poor ball retention in contact, sloppy passing, a lack of aggression and accuracy in making first tackles, and an overall lack of intensity at the end of a marathon season.

But he sees an upside to the downer. 'The scores are amongst the worst I have experienced. It's been painful. However, like all hard-hitting experiences, it is how you deal with them that is the making of you, and I believe this tour will be the making of England's next generation …'

Another significant bonus is that Dallaglio is no yes-man in his relationship with Woodward. He and Johnson share the view that great rugby sides are built on getting the basics right, and that unless Woodward's army of coaches are challenged they can overcomplicate matters with too many classroom sessions.

Dallaglio's authority stems not only from the experience gleaned from two Lions tours and 73 England caps, including 22 as captain, but also from the phenomenal success of Wasps, whom he has captained for eight years. Where other England World Cup winners returned to their clubs and played like shadows of their former selves, the Wasps man was invigorated by his return to the club he has played for as man and boy – despite the demands of virtually two years of non-stop rugby. Dallaglio says that the Wasps coaching team, led by Warren Gatland and Shaun Edwards, have worked a kind of magic by investing training and physical conditioning with huge intensity, but not insisting that it dominates the lives of their players, who get more time off than most of their rivals.

Wasps may not have the resources of Europe's biggest guns, but their focus was laser sharp as Dallaglio led them to superb away victories in the Heineken Cup over Perpignan and Munster, the latter in an epic semi-final, and then to a 27-20 win over Toulouse in a pulsating final at Twickenham to become European champions for the first time. Six days later they secured a memorable double by beating Bath 10-6 to retain the Zurich Premiership title.

Dallaglio has said he would be crazy to let the summer tour defeats wreck what, for him, has been a golden season in which he has won World Cup, European Cup and English Premiership winner's medals. However, as we sat in Singapore airport, he also reiterated that he has never been one for looking back. 'I'll have plenty of time to do that when my playing days are over.'

For the moment, he is savouring every challenge – including the 2005 Lions tour to New Zealand, for which he is a leading contender for the captaincy. 'The England tour has left me with a real motivation to come back … I want another crack at these guys.' The All Blacks have fired Dallaglio's competitive instincts, and that spells danger.

Henry & Jones
Directing the Action

by RAECHELLE EDWARDS

'Henry is experienced, a hard man of the game and many describe him as gruff. Jones, a relative newcomer, could be portrayed as clinical and dispassionate but always definite in his convictions.'

Graham Henry and Eddie Jones are coaches with one similarity – they have both coached a nation other than the one they are native to. Henry coached Wales, and Jones has instructed the Japanese national side. But that is where the similarities start and finish. Henry and Jones are very different people with very different approaches. Henry is experienced, a hard man of the game and many describe him as gruff. Jones, a relative newcomer, could be portrayed as clinical and dispassionate but always definite in his convictions.

With 30 years of coaching experience, Graham Henry is a true professional. He coached the Auckland Blues to championship victories in the Super 12 tournament in 1996 and 1997 and made the final in 1998. Bitterly disappointed at being overlooked again as All Black coach that year, he left New Zealand to take on the role of head coach for Wales. This was a move that angered many Kiwis, particularly rugby administrators from the New Zealand Rugby Union.

'I thought that I'd burnt my bridges when I went to Wales,' Henry reflects. He risked a lot when he turned his back on the land of the long white cloud, but the focused, dedicated and determined Henry was rewarded for this bold move with Welsh victories over England at Wembley and South Africa in Cardiff. Henry also coached Wales to the quarter-finals of the 1999 Rugby World Cup. He then went on to become the first non-British or Irish person to coach the Lions. Success was becoming a habit for the stern Kiwi.

'I've been fortunate enough to coach international rugby for Wales and the British Lions, but there's nothing like coaching your own people and I just feel very fortunate to get the opportunity,' says Henry about his appointment as coach of the All Blacks last year. 'It's always been a lifetime ambition.'

The greatest influence on Henry's coaching career has been former Wales and British Lions coach Carwyn James. 'He coached the British Lions back in 1971. I was starting off as a coach at about that time and it was interesting to see the way that team played. They were much better than the All Blacks in that year and that was a learning curve for me and it was helpful to be able to study what he was doing.'

Henry feels that the experience and knowledge he gained coaching Wales for five years and the Lions has prepared him well for the challenges the All Black coach faces. 'You learn a lot about yourself and you learn other aspects of the game ... you widen your horizons when you coach overseas, you see different styles of play, you deal with a different nationality ... they've got different attitudes,' he says. 'There's also different things you get involved with when you're overseas, there's different media pressures and you don't know the people you are going to coach, so that's a bit of a challenge. And they've got different skill sets to the people you have been used to coaching, so I think it's a big learning experience.'

Henry returned to New Zealand in 2002 and became the technical adviser to the Auckland National Provincial Championship side. He continued this role into 2003 when Auckland won the Ranfurly Shield. He also took up the post as technical adviser to the Auckland Blues Super 12 side that same year, and the team won the Super 12. After the All Blacks failed to make it past the semi-finals of the Rugby World Cup in 2003 Henry finally achieved his goal and replaced John Mitchell as New Zealand's coach. He was appointed for a two-year term. Henry appreciates the national attention, expectation and pressure of the role. He also recognises the impact the All Blacks' results have on the rugby-mad nation. 'What we're trying to do is win and also develop a rugby team, because if you don't win you don't stay, it's as simple as that. Our challenge is to try to keep our head above water while we're developing a rugby team ... a team that's going to be highly competitive on the world stage for a long time.'

Henry's coaching style has evolved from an authoritarian to a democratic style since the 1970s when he began coaching. 'I guess that now the idea is to try to get a group of people together, both management and team, who have an influence on how they play ... you get the best out of a group of people

LEFT Wallaby coach Eddie Jones talks to the press ahead of the Test v England at Brisbane in June 2004.

RIGHT Graham Henry watches his All Blacks beat England at Eden Park the previous week.

PAGE 38 Eddie Jones puts hands-on coaching into practice – Sydney 2004.

ALL BLACKS

by everyone being involved,' he says. 'As a rugby coach it is important that everyone feels that they are part of what you're trying to do ... the players and the management.'

Henry sees the outcomes as a collective responsibility and says his job is to organise people in such a way that they can 'give it their best shot'. The former representative cricketer plans impeccably, stressing the importance of knowing the strengths and weaknesses of opposing teams, explaining, 'a lot of homework needs to be done and every team that you play is different'.

The All Blacks have a relatively young squad, which puts them in a strong position for the World Cup in 2007. Henry believes that older players like Tana Umaga, Carlos Spencer, Justin Marshall and Kees Meeuws may still be playing in three years' time and this will ensure that the squad is robust. 'They are the more senior players, but if they are playing well over the next few years there's no reason why they can't go on to the next World Cup ... I think we've got a problem in this country ... where the guys get to their late 30s and we think they're over the hill and I think that's just a state of mind. If the players are up to it and playing well, whether they are 25 or 35, I don't think it makes a difference. I think we've had an attitude here that once you get into your late 20s you look overseas for an old age pension, to go to Europe or Japan.'

Henry has a close-knit family unit. He is married with two sons who live in New Zealand and a daughter residing in Sydney, Australia. Outside of rugby he likes to relax at the beach, read, travel and go out for dinner with his wife.

Eddie Jones is a different character. Ask mates to describe him and many will say he is 'intense'. Jones has coached the Wallabies for three years and takes this role very seriously. He is a 'purist' and is never satisfied with any performance.

Jones admires two former Australian coaches – Rod Macqueen and Bob Dwyer – and thinks that if you were able to combine these two you would create the perfect coach. 'Rod was a very good thinker about where the game was going; he also put in place in Australian rugby the management principles that have allowed us to sustain success ... Bob was the first coach in Australia to apply scientific principles to rugby training, along with his absolutely great knowledge of the game.'

Jones's rugby-playing career began as a hooker at Matraville High School alongside Wallabies David Knox and the Ella brothers. He then played for the Randwick club in Sydney and also represented New South Wales and the Australian Barbarians, before deciding to concentrate on his career as a teacher and school principal. His first serious coaching step was to take the position of first-grade coach for Randwick. Jones and Dwyer share a strong association with the Randwick club; hence Jones sees his own approach to coaching as similar to Dwyer's methods. The current Wallaby coach considers his style to be 'hands on'.

In 1996 Jones left for Japan to coach the national side, then moved on to the position of head coach at the Suntory Organisation in the Japanese Company Championship. 'I find working in Japan, because it's a different culture, very stimulating for creative thought,' he says. 'What I learnt there is how hard people are able to work ... if you're committed to a course of action, then the discipline and the work ethic that goes with it is certainly evident in Japan.'

Jones believes that 'the one thing that's sometimes forgotten is that no team has become good, and no player has become better, unless they've worked hard'. Jones highlights England's victory in the 2003 Rugby World Cup as an example of this. 'If you look at that four-year period they were consistently the hardest-working team.'

He feels that the Wallabies need to take England's lead on this into their preparation for the next World Cup. 'We've had enormous improvement in that area, the attitude of the players is first class ... we've just got to incrementally improve our work ethic and our work output.' In spite of this focus he understands the importance of balance and variety to ensure the fun and passion still exist, noting that 'when routine becomes mundane you get boredom, and that's when you get a drop-off in the work ethic and the enjoyment out of what you're doing'.

Jones started coaching the ACT Brumbies in 1998. The team finished tenth that year but turned around to make the Super 12 final the year after, losing by a point to the Canterbury Crusaders. In 2001 the Brumbies beat the Sharks in the final by 30 points to win the Super 12 championship. Jones also coached Australia A to victory over the British Lions that year before taking command of the Wallabies. The Wallabies retained the Bledisloe Cup in 2002, and in 2003 defeated the All Blacks in the semi-finals of the Rugby World Cup before being defeated in the dying moments of extra time in a memorable final against England.

Jones is contracted as head coach of the Wallabies until the 2007 Rugby World Cup and is preparing for the event in separate two-year cycles. The period 2004-05 is about 'immediacy and generating high-quality winning performances'. Then the Wallabies will start planning specifically for the World Cup a year out, just as they did for the last tournament. The areas Jones specifically wants to work on include developing a more flexible playing style and concentrating on the strength and power of the team, to build on the aerobic work they have established.

Jones ensures each player gets support from the coaching staff that meets their individual needs. He believes that the week leading up to a Test match involves spending the early part 'getting the physical and tactical side right' and concentrates on the mental aspect of preparation in the later part. He considers knowing the players as well as possible to be vital in this process to ensure all players are in the best possible state to compete in a highly pressured environment.

Jones feels that the only difference in coaching a club team, a Super 12 team and at international level is that everything you do publicly is increasingly scrutinised by the media. Jones tries to minimise this by avoiding spending time in public when he's not working. He has deliberately kept his wife and daughter out of the spotlight. Jones will take Australia into the next World Cup but then plans to move on to a new challenge. He would consider coaching another nation, but only a second-tier country that really needs assistance.

Young Guns
ACT's Rising Stars

by RAECHELLE EDWARDS

'The Brumbies have always given talented youngsters a go. This faith has been rewarded with the discovery and development of many of Australia's finest young talents.'

Since the start of the Super 12 competition, the Brumbies have clearly been the stand-out Australian side. The 2004 tournament was no exception – the ACT-based team won the Super 12 championship, defeating arch-rivals the Canterbury Crusaders 47 points to 38 in the final. The Brumbies ran in five first-half tries in 19 minutes on their way to victory. Twenty-one-year-old winger Mark Gerrard crossed the line three times during the match and fellow youngster Matt Giteau chipped in with his own five-pointer.

The Brumbies have always given talented youngsters a go. This faith has been rewarded with the discovery and development of many of Australia's finest young talents. 'The Brumbies have always been an organisation that has been unencumbered by tradition, because they started with a much freer base than New South Wales and Queensland for professional rugby, and because of that, I think they are keener to take a risk that they think is going to give them a good return,' explains former Brumbies and current Wallaby coach Eddie Jones. 'They've had very good recruitment, they have very good systems in place and I think everyone at the Brumbies has a very clear understanding of how they're going to play the game and therefore the players can develop their skills to play that game.'

The players also have their views on what makes the Brumbies so different. 'I think at the Brumbies we've got the culture where everyone respects each other, the older guys respect the younger guys and the younger guys have the ultimate respect for the older guys,' says 22-year-old scrum half Matt Henjak. 'When you get out there you're playing for each other, no one else ... I think that any team that wins Premierships says that they play for each other, so I think that's the main reason.' New boy South African-born Clyde Rathbone agrees. 'All the boys live within a couple of minutes of each other and it's a really family environment and I think that really contributes to the understanding on the field and I think the facilities and the coaching are at a very high level.'

This year six new players found themselves in the Wallaby squad and all six were from the Brumbies – Rathbone, Gerrard, Henjak, Mark Chisholm, Nic Henderson and Radike Samo. Jones says that it was the appropriate time to introduce new blood to the Wallabies. He feels their

LEFT Mark Gerrard of the Brumbies gets to grips with Crusaders wing Marika Vunibaka in the final of Super 12 2004.

BELOW The young guns swing into town. From left to right, Mark Chisholm, Nic Henderson, Clyde Rathbone, Radike Samo, Mark Gerrard on their induction into the Wallaby squad.

inclusion will add to the talent and enthusiasm of the side with planning already started for Rugby World Cup 2007. The hopes of Wallaby fans rest with these new players and other youngsters like Giteau, who made his national debut two years ago at the age of 20.

Clyde Rathbone played on the right wing for the Brumbies this season, made his Test debut for Australia against Scotland at outside centre, then exploded onto the international rugby stage in Australia's 51-15 emphatic victory over England in Brisbane in June this year. A late injury to Wendell Sailor gave Rathbone a chance on the wing and the flyer made the most of his opportunity to impress, finishing off two first-half tries in a style reminiscent of Ben Tune at his peak. He then backed these up at a crucial moment in the second half with a brilliant solo effort, a grubber and toe ahead to round off his hat-trick of tries against the world champions. 'There's so much competition at the moment for outside backs positions that whenever you get a chance you have to take it,' he says of his dominant performance against England.

Rathbone first gained the interest of rugby scouts in 2002, when he captained South Africa to victory over Australia in the Under 21 Rugby World Cup in Johannesburg. Having played in three Super 12 games for the Sharks in 2002, he was offered a place in the ACT team and moved from his native South Africa. Rathbone suffered with a groin injury in his first season with the Brumbies and didn't make an impact until 2004, when he scored an impressive nine tries based on a game of raw power. 'In this year's Super 12 in the game between the Brumbies and the Bulls in Pretoria I had a pretty good run and I put in a kick for Matt Giteau to score and that sticks out in my mind as one of my better moments,' highlights Rathbone.

He qualifies to play for the Wallabies through his grandmother, who was born in Australia. His parents and three younger brothers still live in Durban, although they plan to emigrate to Australia within the next 12 months. 'Without a doubt [the decision to play for Australia over South Africa] was the toughest decision that I've had to make,' says Rathbone. 'There was no single thing, it was more a combination of factors. I had to weigh up the pros and cons and make a decision. I spoke to Dan Vickerman, he's a guy who's gone through similar things to me, and I used him as a sounding board.'

Rathbone is currently studying small-business management and hopes to one day work for himself. In the meantime he is spending his time away from the game seeing as much of his new country as he can. 'I have lived in Australia for two years now and I consider it home.' This very physical player has signed with Australian Rugby for the next three seasons and will stay with the Brumbies until at least the end of 2005. His versatility is set to keep him in a Wallaby jersey at outside centre or wing over the upcoming seasons. He is very flexible about which position he plays, joking, 'I'll play prop for the team if it's going to get me in the starting line-up!'

After performing well in his first Super 12 season playing for the Brumbies in 2003, Mark Gerrard stepped up in this year's competition, scoring seven tries from the wing. Powerful, fast, with a sidestep, he has his admirers. 'He's a very instinctive footballer, he's got great instinctive skills, he is able to read the game well and along with that he has exceptional footwork,' says Eddie Jones.

Gerrard's rise in Australian rugby has been linear. He made history in Australia as the first player to be contracted to a Super 12 team straight out of school, signing for the Waratahs. Eyeing an opportunity in Canberra, he followed his father's advice. 'Before I moved to the Brumbies my dad sat me down and said I just want you to play and enjoy it, enjoy what you do as long as you can.'

The laid-back apprentice chef has a sporting family, with sister Mo'onia playing for the Australian netball team. Gerrard was elated to be called into the Wallaby squad. 'I was very surprised; you always wish your name will be there in the squad but to actually hear your name being called out and to have the coach ring you to let you know that you are in the team is quite a special feeling,' he comments. This elusive young winger is set to make an impact on the Test arena this year and beyond. His objectives are 'to be the best I can ... try to play as many Tests as I can ... and definitely a goal of mine is to make that squad to play in the next World Cup'.

Nephew of former rugby league player Ivan Henjak, Matt Henjak has started to make his mark on the Australian rugby scene and is hoping to fill the boots George Gregan will leave behind. The Wallaby captain has been a mentor for Henjak, who has played and trained alongside Gregan for the past two seasons. 'I admire George, the way he handles himself on and off the field ... he gave me some advice to always be keen to learn ... always listen and be a sponge and soak everything up,' says the 22-year-old half back. After only one Super 12 cap

LEFT Clyde Rathbone celebrates one of his trio of tries against England at Brisbane – June 2004.

RIGHT Scrum half Matt Henjak in training with the Wallabies at Coffs Harbour – June 2004.

in 2003, Henjak was selected for the Australia A tour of Japan. This season Henjak was a replacement for Gregan in seven Super 12 matches and started against the Otago Highlanders. He made his Test debut against England in Brisbane, playing for the final ten minutes of the match. 'He's a very cheeky half back which is a good attribute to have for a half back,' says Eddie Jones describing Henjak. 'He is a very big half back, he weighs 91 kilograms [14st 4lbs] so he's not dissimilar to Justin Marshall, a good ball runner and a very good organiser around the field.'

He is best mates with his Brumbies and Wallaby team-mate Matt Giteau. 'We have an understanding together, we've grown up living across the road from each other for 14 years, we've always played footy together so I suppose we always knew what each other was doing ... when I play with him we have our little combinations out there and we sort of know what's happening with each other's game.'

The boy from Queanbeyan, with an ultra-competitive nature, is still coming to terms with his inclusion in the national squad. 'It's still a dream ... I sometimes wake up and think "Am I really here?" It's an unbelievable feeling, I really can't explain it.'

The other three new recruits to the Wallabies are forwards. Lock Mark Chisholm caught the eye of the national selectors playing a consistently impressive full Super 12 season this year and scoring six tries, including one particularly outstanding athletic five-pointer against the Queensland Reds. 'He's physically close to one of the best forwards in Australia at the moment, for a young guy that's a pretty big wrap,' Eddie Jones comments. 'He needs to work on his running fitness a bit and because he's so powerful he's a very good ball runner and a very good hitter, so he's potentially a guy who could play No. 6 for Australia.'

The 22-year-old was a member of the Queensland Reds squad in 2002 and made his Super 12 debut for the Brumbies against the Cats in Johannesburg as a replacement in 2003, continuing on to play in another six matches that year. A former Australia Under 19 and Under 21 representative, Chisholm is a physically imposing figure at 197cm (6ft 5½ins) and 112kg (17st 8lbs) and has benefited from training and playing alongside Wallaby locks David Giffin, Justin Harrison and Daniel Vickerman.

Prop Nic Henderson has had the most rapid rise of all of the Wallabies' new recruits. Two years ago he was a back-rower in rugby league, having been contracted to Melbourne Storm straight out

of school. But limited opportunities with the Storm led him to Canberra for a Brumbies Academy Scholarship in 2002 and a spot with Australia Under 21.

Two years on and Henderson started in seven Super 12 matches at tight-head prop, forming a successful front-row partnership with Bill Young and Jeremy Paul. His strong defence, skills and mobility earned him a place in the Australian squad. 'He is a young guy and has only been involved in rugby for two years so his development has been very rapid. He has very good football skills so now he just needs to put on the rugby skills, particularly in terms of scrimmaging, to be the full package,' says Jones.

Radike Samo was born in Fiji and moved to Canberra in 1998. He won a contract with the Brumbies in 2000, but injury and lack of opportunity meant he didn't really make an impression until the 2004 season. This year he featured in every Super 12 match, six in the run-on side.

Samo is a versatile player. The Brumbies used him as a lock this season, but he can also play blind-side flanker or No. 8, and he has even played on the wing in club rugby. He had a stand-out performance against the Waratahs this Super 12 season, marked by physical defence, powerful ball-running out wide and solid skills at the line out and kick-off. He then followed this up with an amazing Super 12 final, which led to his Test debut against Scotland in June 2004.

Jones likes what he sees in the big Fijian. 'He's got exceptional raw ability, he's one of those footballers who is able to do things that other footballers can't do, and he did four significant things at the start of the Super 12 final that resulted in points for the Brumbies … he's big, he's strong, he's fast and he can jump, so they're pretty good qualities for a blind-side flanker.'

Instead of First Class and Business Class, Delta Air Lines offers you BusinessElite® – the business class appreciated by frequent fliers.

How do you describe a level of comfort that lets you step off an eight-hour transatlantic flight feeling more relaxed than when you boarded? Could it be the fact that Delta has removed all middle seats to offer you more space perhaps? Or the generous freedom of movement? Or the way your seat adjusts perfectly to your every wish?

In all probability, it´s all these and more. Because for BusinessElite customers, comfort starts long before they even take their seats, thanks to a special Priority Check-In Service and the spacious Business Lounge. Not to mention the attentive service of our friendly flight attendants.

Then there´s the in-flight cuisine. No, not catering, for this is a different class entirely. Savor an utterly delicious five course menu and you soon forget how high you are flying – or, for that matter, that you are on an aircraft at all. Our award-winning Vinum™ programme is the perfect accompaniment to your food.

And when, over brandy afterwards, you discover the laptop socket in your seat console, you probably won´t even be surprised – though we trust you´ll appreciate it just as much as the personal phone, the large storage space, and the integrated lamp. To round it all off, Delta offers a truly comprehensive entertainment programme with a choice of six films, music and video games for the ultimate in a la carte relaxation.

In France, they say merci. In Germany, it´s danke schoen, in Italy it´s grazie. At Delta Air Lines, we say „150% bonus miles" – our own very special way of saying thank you for choosing to fly BusinessElite. For more information on Delta log on to delta.com or call reservations on 0800 414 767.

INTERNATIONAL SCENE

Rugby At Its Best
International Sevens

by NIGEL STARMER-SMITH

'While Rugby World Cup ... continues to emphasise the gulf between the leading exponents and the rest at fifteen-a-side, those same emerging nations can be, and often are, truly competitive with the "big guns" in the sevens game.'

There seems a reluctance among several of the individual major rugby unions to recognise the appeal, and hence the importance, of the shortened version of fifteen-a-side rugby known as sevens, and in particular the world series of tournaments that go under the banner of the IRB Sevens. Some pay lip service to it, with a modest level of tolerance, and trot out the party line that its usefulness is in providing a proving ground for players of top club and international potential at fifteens. It is certainly that – but so much more besides. Others still see it as it used to be – an end-of-season social frolic; a beery, barbecued hot-dog and hamburger day out for friends and family as

the clubs' posing sleek wing threequarters revel in unaccustomed limelight, running rings around the more rotund, less fleet-of-foot heavyweight forwards who've been roped in to make up the numbers for the British Rail Maintenance RFC Sevens Squad or the Old Shooterhamians. For many a reluctant participant, an afternoon lies ahead of perspiration, humiliation and ultimately agony. No harm in the fun of those occasions either.

But do not confuse the sevens of yesteryear – from the junior club tournament to the erstwhile blue riband events of Melrose and Middlesex – with what is now a thriving international sport in its own right that demands individual fitness levels and skills, athleticism and teamwork that not only match those of fifteens but in certain areas far exceed them. Sevens is not just a cut-down version of rugby, it is a specialist game. What so few understand is that an England sevens squad under Simon Amor or Argentina under Francisco Leonelli, as well as South Africa, New Zealand, Fiji, Samoa, and possibly Scotland, Canada and Kenya too would slaughter any opposition drawn from the international fifteen of any of those same nations. The current national sevens squads are not a 'left-over bunch' on the sidelines of Sir Clive Woodward's or Graham Henry's representative teams. These are specialist professionals in a different sport that deserve a much greater focus of attention than they currently receive – by and large – from their own unions. I say 'by and large' because sevens is already king in the Pacific Islands (Fiji, Tonga, Samoa, Cook Islands, Niue, Papua New Guinea) and is growing dramatically in popularity across the African continent; while in New Zealand – although supercoach Gordon Tietjens is at times thwarted by the power of Super 12, whose clubs understandably swoop to poach young players he has honed into top-class performers – there is a greater well of support than elsewhere.

It is hard to discern the reasons for this reluctant attitude of other individual unions, since without doubt sevens represents the great growth area, in player participation and spectator support, in the worldwide game of rugby. With the advent of the IRB Sevens, the governing body of the sport gave the lead – an annual tournament at the top level, consisting of a world series staged in eight different countries between December and June, plus its own World Cup every four years, to be hosted next in Hong Kong in March 2005.

While Rugby World Cup, the fifteen-a-side tournament, however gripping its final stages, continues to emphasise the gulf between the leading exponents and the rest at fifteen-a-side, those same emerging nations can be, and often are, truly competitive with the 'big guns' in the sevens game. Accordingly it is both surprising and disappointing that the International Olympic Committee have not yet seen fit to introduce sevens into the Olympic Games. Hopefully that day is not too far off. Did the fact not register that the most successful team sport in the Commonwealth Games of both Kuala Lumpur and Manchester when judged by any criteria – crowd attendance, excitement, worldwide participation etc – was rugby sevens? Is there in existence any team sport – and one, I would hasten to add, played by women as well as men – which enjoys the support of national teams in close, meaningful competition on every continent?

A few facts will illustrate the point. Forty nations took part in this season's IRB Sevens. The eight tournaments produced four different winners from four different continents, and never the same winner twice in a row. In Dubai the four-tier competitions of cup, plate, bowl and shield were won by South Africa, Argentina, Canada and Zambia respectively. In Wellington, New Zealand, Tonga, Argentina and the United States took the titles, while in Hong Kong it was England, Scotland and Cook Islands (there was no shield competition).

LEFT Denis Mwanja heads for the try line, receiving instructions all the way, as Kenya beat Australia 29-21 at the Wellington event.

PAGE 51 The Argentinian players and fans celebrate the Pumas' 31-26 victory over the Wallabies in the bowl final in Wellington – February 2004.

No wonder sevens is taking pride of place in so many emerging rugby nations. It is a game in which small rugby nations can be competitive with the best. For most, their lack of player numbers, of facilities, and the absence of the vast human and technical resources that seem to be a prerequisite for success in the international fifteen-a-side game are key factors. Sevens, meanwhile, is easy to learn, uncomplicated and thrilling to watch. All you need is seven players – not fifteen with diverse physical requirements – plus a ball and a patch of beach, scrubland or park for an instant game. And that basic ingredient of running and passing the ball – a scarce commodity at

times in the 'senior' game – is what it is all about. The code is attracting enormous recruitment and great public interest, notably in North America, Africa and Asia. There are 100 sevens tournaments a year in the United States alone.

The clever format of the IRB Sevens tournaments – round-robin pool combinations on the opening day of each competition, with the knockout rounds to follow – gives all nations equal involvement and exposure, favourites mixed in with outsiders, and a learning curve for all. Tournaments have provided regular upsets in recent years that would be unthinkable in the world fifteen-a-side game – for instance Kenya beating Australia, England losing to Korea, the United States, Zimbabwe and Georgia, and even champions New Zealand defeated, as happened this season, by Fiji, France and Argentina.

New Zealand have been the dominant force in the sevens game, but the pack is closing in behind. England took the battle for the overall title to the final tournaments this season and last, while the most recent series saw the rapid emergence of Argentina and South Africa as championship contenders alongside Fiji. But it is lower down the world rankings that the most dramatic rise in standards has been taking place. Teams such as Canada, Kenya, Morocco, Cook Islands, Scotland, Georgia and even Zambia have shown the reality of their challenge to the elite core nations – the top ten who contest every event. The players and coaches cannot fail to gain from the experience of participating alongside the best, and the gaps will continue to close. There are the occasional dramatic upsets of form, while the close encounters between the Goliaths and the Davids increase round by round.

It is important, too, not to ignore the value of the IRB Sevens Series for advancing the standards of the refereeing of the game. With a referee and five supporting officials on touch – or goal – line duty for each tie, the opportunities for up-and-coming officials worldwide to gain from the example set by regular international referees on the circuit, such as South Africa's Craig Joubert, New Zealand's Gary Wise and Wales's Nigel Owens, are boundless. Then there are the discussions on

laws that naturally accompany their coming together off the pitch under the guidance of Steve Griffiths, the IRB Refereeing Co-ordinator.

Nor is it just on the pitch that lessons are learned by players. A unique feature, and one to be cherished, is that all teams live and eat together in the same hotels, and that global mix can only be beneficial for all. While the intensity of the games themselves is unrelenting, the camaraderie away from the action is harmonious and heartwarming. I know of no parallel in team sports.

As for the spectacle itself, there is nothing better to watch than a closely contested sevens game. The individual and collective skills shine forth; the drama is so often intense. And while you may have the occasional one-sided affair, you can be guaranteed that over the course of 44 individual matches in the normal two-day tournament you will have had your fill of thrills and excitement.

This season was no exception. Although New Zealand provided the necessary consistency of performance to retain the overall title for the fifth consecutive year, the outcome was in the balance until the moment that Australia, with the match against New Zealand almost won, failed to clear the ball to touch in the cup quarter-final of the penultimate event, the Emirates Bordeaux Tournament. The kick was sliced and stayed in play, and the New Zealand captain, Liam Messam, set out on a last desperate charge upfield, which three passes later ended in a winning try. So with sufficient tournament points for New Zealand gained from that semi-final place, England were denied any realistic chance of overhauling their rivals before the season's end.

But what a season! Argentina, led by Francisco Leonelli and inspired by the Gomez Cora brothers, won their first ever tournament title, in Los Angeles. South Africa, with so much pace, were always in the top three, until the presence of an ineligible player saw them docked 32 points and fined £100,000 to bring a sad end to a great season. Their outstanding pace overall, spearheaded by Player of the Series Fabien Juries, brought

LEFT George, South Africa, December 2003. Richard Haughton nails South Africa's Danville Demas as England beat the host nation 19-7 in the semi-finals before going on to win the tournament.

RIGHT Twickenham, June 2004. New Zealand lift the IRB Sevens overall trophy for the fifth successive year.

them the Emirates Dubai and Singapore titles. England were mostly superb but fell from grace twice, in Los Angeles and Singapore, when Simon Amor's squad were out of sorts, with injuries, illness and uncharacteristic errors ultimately denying them the title that was in their sights. Even so, they were alone in winning three tournaments – the Emirates South African and London events, plus, for the third consecutive time, Hong Kong.

Amor himself and Ben Gollings at half back were the architects of England's triumphs, with Gollings finishing as leading points scorer for the series. Rob Thirlby has never played better, and the top try scorer award shared with Juries was just reward. Richard Haughton and Ugo Monye were the 'gas men', repeatedly outflanking the opposition, but it was Tony Roques, Phil Dowson and Pat Sanderson who did the graft in tight and loose to create the vital possession for England to use. Pete Richards when called on quickly proved his worth – and future prospects in the sport – as support to either half back. And as for Henry Paul – when available – he was instrumental with his power and perception in securing England's triumphs in both Hong Kong and London, and left not only me wondering why his recall to England's fifteen-a-side squad has never happened.

With his call-up to assist Sir Clive Woodward, Joe Lydon stepped down after taking England to unprecedented levels of performance in his three-year stint as coach; he presided over a magnificent transformation, aided along the way by team manager John Elliott. But Mike Friday – a fine sevens exponent in his playing days with Blackheath and Wasps and formerly Lydon's assistant – quickly showed his ability to continue England's forward march as he guided the side to the Twickenham title.

A new eight-tournament IRB series gets under way in December, opening with the Emirates Dubai event. Of course, the focal point of the sevens game will be the World Cup in Hong Kong in March, with the destiny of that title wide open as New Zealand defend their crown. If you're able to get there, don't miss an event on the world sevens circuit. I promise you you'll not regret it. Crowds of 43,500 in Wellington, 45,000 in Hong Kong and a full house of 25,000 in Dubai will tell you the same. Why it is that other major host unions seem to lack the will or promotional skill to similarly fill their stadiums is a question that requires an answer. The cut and thrust of sevens, the truly global game of rugby, is riveting entertainment – and fun, on and off the field, is guaranteed!

Future Perfect
IRB Under 21 World Championship

by ALAN LORIMER

'What put New Zealand out in front, however, was the sheer class of their players – out and out stars of the game at Under 21 level. The power, pace and panache of their back line made a massive impression on the tournament ...'

Whatever the fallout from New Zealand's Rugby World Cup failure in Australia, the All Blacks' successes at age-group level last season will surely have provided the antidote to any residual despondency. In an all-conquering year New Zealand captured the IRB world titles at both Under 19 and Under 21 to suggest that the All Blacks' assembly line is back on full power.

Of course it can be argued that Under 19 rugby is not an accurate predictor of later success at senior level, but that is certainly not true of the Under 21 game. The Under 21 championship is the place to observe the stars of tomorrow. Or as the logo of the 2004 championship in Scotland put it – 'Rugby's Future. Now'.

New Zealand were always going to be favourites to lift the Under 21 title this year following their success with a young squad in the 2003 championship, staged in England. In the event they won comfortably, producing on the way sensational performances that are now the benchmark for all future aspiring sides.

From a rugby standpoint it was the overall quality that made the 2004 championship such a success. 'The standard has gone up again. There was a big increase last year from the year before but it's even higher this year,' admitted Bryce Woodward, the New Zealand Under 21 coach.

What put New Zealand out in front, however, was the sheer class of their players – out and out stars of the game at Under 21 level. The power, pace and panache of their back line made a massive impression on the tournament, especially in the final, where, despite the wet conditions at Hughenden in Glasgow, New Zealand threatened every time they moved the ball wide.

Few will forget the midfield combination of Stephen Donald at outside half, Luke McAlister at inside centre and the already capped Ben Atiga in the No. 13 position. Then there was the devastating finishing of the final's triple try-scoring wing, Tony Koonwaiyou; the defence-splitting running of full back and Super 12 player Glen Horton; and the hugely impressive Jerome Kaino at No. 8, another Super 12 player, who looks destined for higher honours.

If New Zealand finished in their expected number one position, then few anticipated that the runners-up would be Ireland. Seeded seventh, Ireland proceeded to contradict the forecasts with a run of four wins over Tonga, Argentina, France and Australia, before losing to New Zealand in the final. Ireland's success was all about synergy. Sure, they had a few players in their side who will make the grade at senior level, but you got the distinct impression that the whole exceeded the sum of the parts by a big margin. 'This is an Ireland team that really plays for one another,' said Ireland manager Dave Haslett, whose side became the first team from north of the equator to challenge the dominance of the southern hemisphere.

Outstanding for Ireland were No. 8 Jamie Heaslip, outside half Gareth Steenson (who finished as the tournament's top points scorer), lock Dave Gannon, prop Declan Fitzgerald and centres John Hearty and Glen Telford. One who would surely have featured in this list was Tommy Bowe, but sadly for the player and for Ireland, a shoulder injury ended his tournament after the second round.

Winners two years ago, South Africa were seeded fourth but finished satisfyingly one notch up. Many felt that South Africa, with four established Super 12 players in their squad, looked the silver medallist side, but the vagaries of the tournament, which resulted in them meeting New Zealand twice, ended that possibility. South Africa had recognised stars in outside half Derick Hougaard, flanker Luke Watson, full back Hendrik Daniller and wing Marius Delport, but a number of others showed up well, among them inside centre Wynand Olivier, lock Andries Bekker – who at 2.08m (6ft 10ins) is the tallest player in South Africa – and outside back Bryan Habana, a player with clever feet and great pace.

Runners-up last year, Australia dropped to fourth ranking after losing their last two matches to Ireland and South Africa. Still, the exercise was worth it, especially if the talents of centre Chris Siale are seen in Super 12 rugby next season. Another young Wallaby to watch is flanker Lei Tomiki, whose play is reminiscent of current Australia back-row forward George Smith.

It was Six Nations Under 21 champions England who were expected to head the northern hemisphere challenge. In fact the seeding committee got it right when they ranked them fifth, but England might feel aggrieved that they failed to make the top four despite finishing with four wins and only one loss. This is one of the quirks of a tournament which, for practical reasons, is necessarily truncated. What is missing is a quarter-final round to iron out any seeding anomalies. The lack of it meant that New Zealand and South Africa met twice, as did England and Wales. Had the top eight from the pool stages gone into quarter-finals then England would have met South Africa, Wales would have faced Australia, and so on.

England, who effectively lost sevens star Ugo Monye before the tournament started, were a shade unfortunate to meet New Zealand in the opening round. They needed at least one point from this game, but in the event failure here and their inability to score four tries against both Scotland and Wales cost them a place in the top four.

Still, at Under 21 level it is the spin-off that is important, and in this context England will be pleased with the progress of several of the squad. 'A number of players like Chris Bell, Tom Rees, Geoff Parling, Nick Wood and James Percival have had a good tournament. It's now up to them to establish themselves in the English Premiership,' said England manager Pete Drewett.

Chasing England closely were Wales, who eventually finished sixth after matching England in the final game on tries but losing to their UK rivals on points. Wales, however, have youth on their side, and with the bulk of their squad back for next year's IRB Under 21 World Championship, it all looks promising for the Welsh team. Among the returnees will be Gavin Quinnell, the youngest of the famous rugby-playing brothers but a relative newcomer to rugby. 'Gavin, in spite of or maybe because of his famous family, concentrated on golf. He's probably two years behind where he should be. But he's proved to be a great ball carrier for us,' said Wales head coach Chris Davey.

One place behind Wales were Argentina, who failed to live up to their third seeding. The young Pumas were only just defeated by second-placed Ireland, but setbacks against England and Australia meant that Argentina would finish in the middle four. What went wrong is difficult to say. Certainly there was no lack of talent, half backs Alfredo Lalanne and Alfredo Cordone being the best on view, but somehow the whole was less than the sum of the parts.

Equally disappointing in the 2004 tournament were France, who had to settle for eighth place. The warning signs were there when Italy ran France desperately close in the pool stage, but it was the defeats by Ireland and then Wales that torpedoed the French challenge.

In the bottom four it was Italy who emerged top after comfortably defeating hosts Scotland in the final match at New Anniesland to reverse the result between the countries in the Six Nations Under 21 Championship. Of course it helped having senior international Mirco Bergamasco in the squad, but with talent like scrum half Giulio Toniolatti, sharpshooting kicker Andrea Marcato and skilful flanker Robert Barbieri in the side Italy were bound to threaten.

For host country Scotland this was always going to be a difficult tournament without the professional experience of their top two Under 21s, Tom Philip and Ally Hogg, and without skipper David Callam for all but half a game. Moreover, Scotland's small playing numbers at this level meant that the bulk of their squad was chosen from amateur clubs, galaxies away from the Super 12 and Premiership players of other countries.

Even so, the performance of the Scotland squad was far below the standards laid down by the management, causing coach Iain Paxton to castigate his charges. 'A lot of these players should take a long hard look at themselves and what they're producing,' he said. Notwithstanding their tenth-place finish, Scotland can at least look to players like scrum half Mark McMillan, prop Alasdair Dickinson, hooker Fergus Thomson and flanker Alasdair Strokosch to challenge for senior places.

In eleventh position, Russia, who have shown up well in international sevens and at Under 19 level, gave further evidence that their game is prospering. Foreign club scouts would have noted scrum half Yury Kushnarev and a mountain of muscle in Russia's powerhouse pack.

It was never going to be easy for Tonga in this company, but the South Sea islanders showed flair throughout, and in winger Alaska Taufa had a player of natural ability.

The Scotland-staged tournament showed us where rugby is going. It pointed to greater physique, better conditioning and sharper skills. It also confirmed the view that, France apart, the northern hemisphere sides are still behind in creative back play.

Overall the 2004 championship was a huge success, not least because of the marketing effort that resulted in record crowds (47,500) turning out to watch quality rugby. 'Commercially this tournament surpassed our expectations,' said Scottish Rugby's chief executive, Phil Anderton. 'It laid to rest the ghost of the '99 World Cup and showed that Scotland is capable of staging major sporting events,' he added.

The 2005 IRB Under 21 World Championship will be staged in Argentina. You can bet that standards will again rise, players will be even fitter and stronger, and that fancy footwork will not be just the preserve of tango dancers.

A Game to Remember
the 1924 Olympic Rugby Final

by CHRIS THAU

'With a humiliating French defeat imminent, the crowd went wild and began to attack the American supporters in the stand and even the players on the field. The match finished in pandemonium with the public throwing stones and bottles ...'

Eighty years ago, on 18 May 1924, rugby was played for the last time in the Olympic Games. At the instigation of the French Federation and with the support of the International Board, the occasion was commemorated last May at the newly launched Bordeaux Sevens Tournament, part of the IRB Sevens Series. Appropriately it was the students of Bordeaux University, who so enthusiastically started playing *le Jeu Anglais* more than a century ago, who re-enacted the historic match between France and the United States. The playing kit was specifically designed for the event, the jerseys and referees' blazers having been manufactured by the company run by former England No. 8 John Scott.

Rugby had been played previously at three other Olympic Games – at the II Olympiad in Paris in 1900, when France won the gold; in 1908 in London, when the touring Wallabies became Olympic champions; and in 1920 in Antwerp, when the United States, featuring a selection of Californian students, managed to defeat France 8-0 to win the first of their Olympic gold medals.

The games of the VIII Olympiad commenced on 4 May 1924 and lasted nearly three months, the closing ceremony taking place on 27 July. Among the 3,092 athletes from 44 countries competing in 17 sports, there were some 60-odd rugby players representing host nation France, reigning Olympic champions the United States and Romania, who were making their debut in the international arena.

The Olympic rugby competition began on the opening day with the match between hosts France, captained by veteran No. 8 René Lasserre of Grenoble, who had made his international debut against Ireland ten years earlier before the Great War, and Romania, captained by ageing centre Nicolae Marascu. Not unexpectedly the experienced and powerful French despatched the newcomers from Eastern Europe by a record 61 points to 3 – according to some sources the score was actually 59-3 – scoring a record 13 tries in the process, including four (also a French record) from the famous winger Adolphe Jaureguy. The walkover win must have given the French players and public false expectations, which were exacerbated by an intense and partisan media campaign.

On the following Sunday, 11 May, the United States, captained by full back Charlie Doe, comprehensively defeated Romania, once again led by Nicolae Marascu, at Stade Colombes, Paris. The Americans scored eight tries for a final scoreline of 39-0. Richard Hyland claimed four (a US record), and Jack Patrick, playing at flanker, scored a hat-trick. The 5,000 French crowd supported Romania, but the Eastern Europeans were thoroughly outplayed by their bigger, faster, stronger and, to the surprise of the French, more skilful opponents, setting the scene for the final showdown against the French the following weekend. The defeat ended Romania's campaign in the Olympics, but secured them the bronze, the country's first-ever Olympic medal.

The Olympic final was played at Stade Colombes on 18 May 1924 before a strongly partisan crowd of about 50,000. The exceedingly generous odds of the local bookmakers – 5-1 for a straight French win – reflected the general state of euphoria in the aftermath of the Romanian game and no doubt had influenced the mindset of the French team.

The US captain was No. 8 Colby Slater of the University of California, Berkeley, one of the seven 1920 gold medallists in the US squad, while the French were once more led by René Lasserre. The

American team wore white V-neck jerseys adorned with the shield of All American Student Rugby, white shorts and white socks with red and blue hoops. France wore their traditional blue jerseys with white shorts and blue socks.

The Americans, who won the toss, used an aspect of the laws to maximise what they thought was their superior fitness and stamina. At the time of the Olympics the length of a match was variable, with the toss-winning captain having the privilege of requesting the length of time to be played. Despite the protestations of the French, Slater asked referee Albert Freethy to play 45 minutes each way, hoping that the US team's fitness would see them through. He was to be vindicated.

It is quite clear that the Americans targeted Jaureguy, who was perceived as the main threat. The tackle law was vague at the time, and the flying tackles of American football, with their devastating velocity, could do considerable damage. Two minutes into the game, as the French flyer set off for the American line he was flattened by an American-football-style bone-crushing tackle from William Rogers, who was Stanford University's basketball captain. Soon afterwards, with Jaureguy once more in full flight, Rogers struck again and rattled the Frenchman. Finally lock forward Alan Valentine, the only US player residing in England – he was studying at Oxford University – hit Jaureguy so hard that the French winger was carried off bleeding and was unable to resume.

While in the first half the French seemed able to absorb nearly everything the Americans threw at them, after the break, and reduced to 14 men, the French defence eventually crumbled under the

relentless onslaught. The Americans added four more tries to their 3–0 half-time lead, with Henri Galau scoring France's solitary try for a final scoreline of 17–3. This match ended the careers of several French players, including that of skipper Lasserre, who never played for France again.

With a humiliating French defeat imminent, the crowd went wild and began to attack the American supporters in the stand and even the players on the field. The match finished in pandemonium with the public throwing stones and bottles at the players and with one of the US reserve players, Gideon Nelson, flattened by a walking stick.

At its 1925 Congress, the International Olympic Committee (IOC) decided to end rugby's association with the Olympic Games, despite vigorous protestations from Dutch students keen to have rugby in the programme of the 1928 Olympic Games in Amsterdam. The decision of the founder of the Olympics, Baron Pierre de Coubertin – himself a keen supporter of rugby – to step down as president of the IOC at the 1925 Congress removed the last remaining obstacle in the way of those demanding the exclusion of rugby from the Olympic programme.

BELOW Bordeaux University players line up to commemorate the re-enactment of the 1924 Olympic final. In the first row at centre is referee Albert Freethy (played by local Bordeaux referee Christophe Maltère), flanked by American captain Colby 'Babe' Slater and French skipper René Lasserre. Touch judges Cyril Rutherford, of the French Federation, and Norman Slater, brother of the US captain, are here played respectively by Bordeaux referees Jean-Louis Filon and Richard Denninger.

Seek inspiration within

Discover Hong Kong with the airline that knows it best

Cathay Pacific flies three times a day non-stop from Heathrow to Hong Kong – that's more than any other airline. With connections to 34 cities in Asia, China, Australia and New Zealand, there's no better way to experience the East.

Now you're really flying.

www.cathaypacific.com

CATHAY PACIFIC

Rugby Without Frontiers
the Game in Africa

by CHRIS THAU

'The whole session moved into overdrive when the technical director of the Côte d'Ivoire Federation, Marc Panebiere, one of the two match commissioners in Lomé, joined the fray teaching the kids some fun games with the ball.'

The decision of Olivier Gau, an Air France flight attendant, to register a new charity, Rugby sans Frontières, with the Paris Prefecture last July was triggered by an unexpected encounter with African rugby during a trip to Lomé, the capital of Togo in West Africa, the week before. Gau – initially excited by the discovery of an international tournament involving the local team, Togo, and their neighbours Benin, Nigeria and Ghana – was bowled over by the enthusiasm of the local kids, coached by Hugo Agbanama on one of the endless sandy beaches of Lomé.

'It was fabulous to watch international rugby in Lomé, but the day I spent on the beach with Hugo and his kids was something really special. This revealed to me how important a rugby ball could be in Africa – not to mention rugby kit – and having spoken to my team-mates from Air France Rugby Club we decided to form a charity to help the African children and any other children in poor countries to play rugby. It is as simple as that,' said Gau, who once played for Racing Club de France.

The matches between Ghana and Benin and Nigeria and Togo in Lomé ended a week of rugby action; part of what the Confederation of African Rugby (CAR) grandly calls the Super 16 competition – the second division of the All-Africa Championship in all but name. The launch of the

competition has been a catalyst for dormant African rugby. Suddenly a host of rugby nations such as Ghana, Burkina Faso, Mali, Burundi, Togo, Tanzania and Benin emerged almost overnight and out of nowhere, launching themselves into action with an enthusiasm and passion that defied their limited skill and experience.

Unfortunately the first Super 16 competition, held last autumn in Bamako in Mali and Lusaka in Zambia, was overshadowed by the glitter of RWC 2003 in Australia and hardly made any headlines outside Africa. However, while ignored by the world of rugby the competition managed to ignite the imagination of the African nations keen to compete internationally, with Cameroon, winners of the Northern pool, defeating Zambia, winners of the Southern pool, 15-12 in the final.

The Super 16 competition is the brainchild of the current president of the CAR – one Abdelazizi Bougja, a dynamic former Moroccan international centre who lives and works in Paris. 'In the majority of the 30-odd CAR member unions rugby has been played on and off for some 20-30 years, mostly by expatriates; unlike South Africa, Morocco, Tunisia, Zimbabwe and Namibia where the game is well established. What caught the imagination of the African nations in my view was the success of Côte d'Ivoire, who reached the 1995 RWC finals. That was the turning point,' Bougja said.

PAGE 63 Olivier Gau (left) and Hugo Agbanama with the first development group of Togolese children.

BELOW Super 16 captains pose in Dakar in front of a protected 500-year-old African baobab tree. From left to right: Senegal's Adma Bakhoum, Mali's Ali Diarra, SRF president Guedel Ndiaye, Burkina Faso's Amed Coulibaly, Mauritania's Alioune Abdoulaye Ba.

'International sport is what makes Africa tick and for many African countries, the incentive and the desire to compete internationally, within an All-Africa context, is very strong, although their domestic game is very much in an embryonic stage. Generally it is difficult to decide at what stage in the development of a nation they are ready for international competition. In Africa, a national team, involved in an official international competition, acts as a locomotive for the

domestic game. I have no doubt that many of the new African unions, who are not even members of the IRB yet, will expand their development based on their budding international programme. It is like building a house starting with the roof, but this is the reality of Africa and we must understand it and use it if we want to make progress. Not to mention what will happen when rugby becomes an Olympic sport again. I am sure this will have an extraordinary impact on African rugby.'

'Development in Africa,' observed Jean-Luc Barthes, the IRB development manager for French-speaking Africa, 'is an uneven phenomenon which differs in terms of size, approach and style from country to country. The key here is finding the right balance between international exposure and genuine domestic development. The wealth of talent and enthusiasm in the new African nations is huge, but we must guide their growth with due care and attention to enable them to fulfil their international ambitions, while building up a sound infrastructure, in most cases literally from scratch, in countries where poverty is endemic and shortages are a way of life. A rugby ball in Africa is a huge resource, but by the same token African governments do get involved when the national team is representing the country.'

In Togo, where rugby has taken off following the election of 38-year-old former international hooker Modeste Akossan as federation president, international rugby is key to recognition. 'We have about 250 players in five clubs in Lomé, one in Sokodé, which is my original club, and three others ... but until and unless the Togolese Rugby Federation is accepted by the Togolese Olympic Committee as a legitimate member we will not make progress. And the chances for that are quite good, I am told, after the Athens Olympics,' he said.

Adom Abotchi, director of cabinet of the Togo Minister for Youth and Sport, confirmed, in his role as technical director of the Togolese Olympic Committee, that Togo rugby was in line for Olympic recognition after the 2004 Olympic Games. 'There is no question that rugby fulfils all criteria for admission and I cannot foresee any problem at the next meeting of the Togolese Olympic Committee after the Olympics. Rugby has a good playing ethics, it has strong educational values, it has a sound infrastructure and our teams play it internationally,' he said.

While Togo has been playing international rugby, admittedly on an ad hoc basis, against its neighbours for some years now, development is very much in its infancy. Togo men are big and muscular and enjoy physical contact sport, while the kids, like everywhere else in the world, love running with the ball. What Akossan did in the aftermath of Togo's disappointing campaign in the Bamako tournament last year was to talk his team-mate and protégé Hugo Agbanama into starting a development programme in Lomé. Agbanama, whose career as a scrum half was cut short by injury, studies telecommunications at the local university, sponsored by Akossan himself, who is the owner of a large telecommunications company.

'After Bamako, I started recruiting kids straightaway. I went to their parents, explained what rugby was all about. They were all concerned about the physical aspects of the game, but I managed to allay their fears. This is how I started, and now I have over 60 children to look [out] for, from Under 9 to Under 18,' said Agbanama, who is coaching the entire development group from minis to Under 18s.

Gau and Agbanama struck up an instant friendship, with the Air France man taking over the coaching of the minis while the student from Lomé concentrated on his Under 18 charges in preparation for the first All-Africa Under 18 Championship, also launched this year. The whole session moved into overdrive when the technical director of the Côte d'Ivoire Federation, Marc Panebiere, one of the two match commissioners in Lomé, joined the fray teaching the kids some fun games with the ball.

Development in Ghana, explained union president Mrs Gifty Annan-Myers, is very much led by the national team, and following the formation of this team, with the expert help of Cameroon player Charly Kamgana, the government is prepared to help. In Nigeria, the sleeping giant of Africa, the game is taking off in a big way, with rugby officially included among the sports of the country's National Sports Festival for the first time, says Ntiense Williams, technical director of the Nigerian Rugby Association.

Development in Mali, winners of the Dakar Super 16 tournament, has a different complexion. 'It is early days, but there is a great deal of talent and love for the game in a country where there is a tradition for teamwork and collective ethic,' said Jean-François Beliers, the team No. 8 and a farming expert. The country's sports officials have noted the success in the Dakar tournament at the end of June, and rugby has been targeted as a growth sport for the future, confirmed Ahmed Sekou-Touré, director general in the Ministry of Sport in Mali, who watched his team prevail in a tightly fought final over a talented Senegal team at Iba Mar Diop Stadium in Dakar.

Most remarkable, though, is the development programme launched by the Senegalese Rugby Federation – one of the few full IRB members in the Super 16 – on a French Federation blueprint in a number of centres around Dakar. The pilot projects are Ecole de Rugby de Pikine et Guediawaye, Ecole de Rugby Liberté 4, and Ecole de Rugby de Rufisque. The last is in a coastal fishing village that is the headquarters of the Espadons Rugby Club. The centre and the club are run by wing forward Mansour Mbaye, one of Senegal's leading international players, with the assistance of Mamadou Dia, one of the local kids turned assistant coach. The various pilot projects are co-ordinated by 52-year-old police inspector Biram Kébé, a former international player, who strongly believes in the educational values of rugby. The Senegal development programme is sponsored by the Senegalese Rugby Federation president, Guedel Ndiaye, a distinguished Dakar lawyer and a former captain of his country, together with the federation secretary, Jean-Martin Jampy, who is the communications director of a large cement multinational operating from Dakar, and it is supported by a group of passionate people of likeminded disposition, chief among them Syndieli Wade, the daughter of the Senegalese Republic's president.

Meanwhile, the winners of the four Super 16 pools are set to cross swords in the semi-finals in the autumn, with Mali, winners of Pool A in Dakar, taking on Nigeria, who prevailed over Togo to finish top in Pool B in Lomé, and Tanzania, the likely winners of Pool D, playing either Botswana or Swaziland, who are battling for honours in Pool C. Given their playing standard and experience, it looks as if either Botswana or Swaziland will secure the Super 16 crown, although the newly launched Nigerian team may well be in contention.

BELOW Line-out practice in progress at Ecole de Rugby de Pikine et Guediawaye, near Dakar, Senegal.

Summer Tours 2004
England in New Zealand and Australia
by DAVID HANDS

'So it was that a weary England squad, weakened by retirement and injury, dragged themselves onto the flight for Auckland ... to offer themselves as cannon fodder to southern hemisphere giants indignant at the loss of the Webb Ellis Cup.'

So, 2003-04, the Jekyll and Hyde season for England. And of that season, which in playing terms started on 23 August and ended the following 26 June, the most monstrous part was the last three weeks, when England took their World Cup-winning reputation back to the southern hemisphere and left it in tatters on the fields of Dunedin, Auckland and Brisbane.

It was hard not to believe, for all the assurances to the contrary, that England achieved their heart's desire in Sydney on 22 November, when they won the World Cup, and everything that followed was mundane by comparison. But whoever conceived the notion that returning to play New Zealand twice and Australia at the fag end of the season might possibly have been a good idea deserves to be taken out and shot.

International fixtures and tour schedules these days seem to follow a quid pro quo regime and a financial imperative, but it was interesting to observe that England and France, neck and neck as northern hemisphere challengers for the 2003 World Cup, had totally different end-of-season tours – England to Australasia; France to North America. So it was that a weary England squad, weakened by retirement and injury, dragged themselves onto the flight for Auckland at the beginning of June to offer themselves as cannon fodder to southern hemisphere giants indignant at the loss of the Webb Ellis Cup.

Apart from the departure of Martin Johnson, Neil Back, Kyran Bracken, Jason Leonard, Dorian West and Paul Grayson from international rugby, injury deprived Sir Clive Woodward of Jonny Wilkinson, Lewis Moody, Phil Vickery, Alex Sanderson, Graham Rowntree and Ollie Smith. Throw in Will Greenwood and Ben Kay, whose form had patently declined, and the agreement to leave Jason Robinson at home for his first complete summer off since 1992, and the potential for a fall from grace was obvious.

Not that it necessarily seemed that way as the first clash with the All Blacks at Carisbrook loomed. New Zealand had undergone something of a transition since the World Cup, with a new coaching panel who appointed a new captain and then watched a trial match in which their favoured XV was hustled from pillar to post and sneaked home with a one-point win. A comparison of the two forward packs favoured England heavily, with three times the number of caps and a wealth of experience, even if the New Zealand back division looked by far the more threatening than an English line prepared for the first time by Joe Lydon, the new attack coach.

But experience counts for nothing if it is not applied. Far too many England players had no recent form behind them. Those who had – individuals such as Joe Worsley and Martin Corry, who ended the domestic season so strongly for London Wasps and Leicester respectively – were ignored. England travelled short of an open-side flanker and found themselves even shorter when Bath's Michael Lipman pulled up in training. So Richard Hill, world class on the blind side but not to be compared with New Zealand's vice captain, Richie McCaw, in a No. 7 jersey, filled the void.

Elsewhere Steve Thompson, Matt Dawson, Ben Cohen, Mike Tindall and Mike Catt were either short of form or rugby and, with the notable exception of the courageous Tindall in the centre, played like it. For all that, it was hard to comprehend a first half in which New Zealand not only scored 30 points but dominated the forward exchanges utterly. Graham Henry, the former Wales and British Lions coach who took over the All Blacks from John Mitchell after the World Cup, had emphasised a 'return to basics' approach and called up forwards relatively unknown outside New Zealand such as Jono Gibbes, Keith Robinson and Carl Hayman.

Not only did they hold their own in the scrums, they dominated the line out and ruled in the loose, where England turned over ball with alarming regularity. Moreover, the defence in which England took such pride throughout 2003 collapsed against a side prepared to trust the speed and ball-handling of their backs. From the moment that Joe Rokocoko ran back England's kick-off, making 40 metres past three flailing tackles, New Zealand held the whip hand.

Tries by Carlos Spencer, Rokocoko and Doug Howlett were all converted by Daniel Carter, the inside centre, who in the course of two internationals kicked 13 goals out of 13. If England lost the second half by no more than 6-3, that was doubtless because New Zealand knew they had the game in hand and were no doubt congratulating themselves at running the world champions ragged.

Woodward, the head coach, acknowledged afterwards that England had been 'ambushed', but worse was to follow in the second international, at Auckland's Eden Park. Simon Shaw, the Wasps lock, became the third player in England's international history to be sent off (following Mike Burton against Australia in 1975 and Danny Grewcock against New Zealand in 1998), and Grewcock was subsequently cited for foul play less than a minute after he came on as a second-half replacement.

Shaw's dismissal, for kneeing Robinson in the back at a ruck only ten minutes into the game, left England conducting a damage-limitation exercise. Seen with the naked eye, the incident seemed hardly worth a yellow card, falling as it did into the category of a physical 'warning' to a player on the wrong side of the ruck; Shaw himself described it as a 'clumsy' way of rucking. Several New Zealand commentators felt the red card was undeserved, but given the advice he received from Stuart Dickinson, his Australian touch judge, the referee from Wales, Nigel Williams, had little option but to dismiss Shaw.

At the disciplinary hearing the following day, Shaw escaped further censure on a technicality, in that the referee had taken advice from the video referee – another Australian, Matt Goddard – for purposes of identification. Though this is permitted in Sanzar competitions, it is not under International Rugby Board regulations, leaving England's QC, Richard Smith, able to free Shaw for service the following Saturday. Grewcock, though, was suspended for six weeks for stamping on Carter, a punishment which prevented him playing against Australia but thereafter only affected his pre-season games for Bath going into 2004-05.

It was little comfort for England, who conceded 36 points for the second week running against a New Zealand side deprived by injury of McCaw and Howlett. When Shaw was sent off they were leading 6-0 and looked far more competitive than in Dunedin. They turned round no more than 10-6 in arrears, but that was before Rokocoko stamped his mark on the game. The lithe Auckland wing scored three tries, the product both of his own elusive running and of the accuracy of the passing of his inside backs. Charlie Hodgson's goal-kicking kept England in touch, until Rokocoko's third try and a final score from Spencer left them down and out.

Any faint hope that England could hold Australia at Brisbane's Suncorp Stadium died at the hands and feet of Clyde Rathbone, the South African-born wing who was not even due to play. Australia, inevitably, advertised the encounter as the 'rematch' of the World Cup final, even though England started with no more than five survivors from that game. Australia boasted 12, though that was reduced to 11 when Wendell Sailor strained a hamstring during the pre-match warm-up and conceded his place on the right wing to Rathbone.

Again, England started relatively well, but by half-time Rathbone had scored two tries and Australia led 21-8 despite limited possession. England's persevering play produced tries for Hill and Lawrence Dallaglio, the second of which pulled them back to 24-15. But the back play was laboured, and whenever England put together any sustained passages of play, they invariably ended with a turnover or a penalty to Australia. The final quarter, after Rathbone had completed his treble with a spectacular chip-and-chase try, turned into a rout – England conceded three further tries and, for good measure, Joe Roff kicked a penalty goal five minutes into injury time to make the final score 51-15. It was the third-highest defeat England have suffered, after the 76-0 thrashing in the same stadium in 1998 and the 64-22 loss to New Zealand that same year.

Amid the plethora of mistakes on the field and off, there were hints from such players as Hodgson, Olly Barkley and Tom Voyce that they will serve England well in the future. But the next generation of England forwards did not put their hands up. Dallaglio and Worsley played as well as circumstances allowed, and their club colleague Tim Payne made a debut remarkable for the fact that, within a month, he won a winner's medal in the Heineken Cup and the Zurich Premiership and then played for England after spending most of the season as second-choice loose-head prop for Wasps behind Craig Dowd.

The reckoning will come when England play Australia at Twickenham in November, but the result of that match will not alter the fact that England's stock, so high in global terms after winning the World Cup, declined sadly in 2004. It was, in all ways, a tour too far.

BELOW A little light in the darkness for England as skipper Lawrence Dallaglio goes over for his side's second try against the Wallabies in Brisbane.

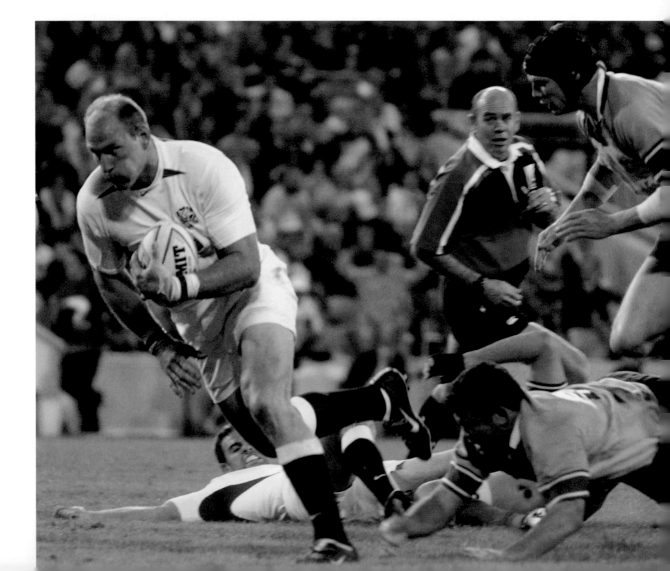

The Churchill Cup

by TERRY COOPER

"'It's a vital tournament for Canada and the US and especially for us now that we don't have the Six Nations A-team Championship in Europe any more.'"

Hugh Vyvyan's England squad in Canada – roughly a 3rd XV – narrowly failed to win the Churchill Cup (and to shed what would have been a single candle's worth of consolation) on the same day that Lawrence Dallaglio's Test team were 'blackwashed' in Auckland by the All Blacks. The ambitious squad, coached again by Sale's Jim Mallinder, went down in extra time to New Zealand Maori. It was a different but almost as frustrating a loss as the seniors' 14-man defeat in the real Test match.

ABOVE Pat Sanderson in action during the 48-23 win over Canada. A member of England's sevens squad, Sanderson has moved from Quins to Worcester for 2004-05.

There were 18 hours between the two games because of the time difference, so Vyvyan's team had plenty of time to reflect that not too many people in the Dallaglio party were doing themselves too many favours and that Sir Clive Woodward might be seeking to remedy any growing weaknesses. The same had applied the week before when England faced Canada in the semi-final after absorbing news of England's first-Test defeat. Could the next generation bang the drum? Not hard enough! They played some delectable rugby in the opening half against the Maori, but the England half of the scoreboard rusted over after 37 minutes, when it had shown a 19-5 lead, and the legs turned to asparagus as the clock ticked beyond the 100-minute mark.

Mallinder and forwards' coach Steve Diamond took 27 players on tour – 16 uncapped, with the remaining 11 having a mere 35 caps between them. These visits to North America have been a feature of this century. In 2003 England won the cup, but this time the entry of the Maori turned the week into a four-nation event. Mallinder stated the obvious objective: 'Our aim is to retain the cup and try to ensure that the trickle of players who emerge from these trips as ready-made Six Nations operators is turned into a steady flow. The players are eyeing up their prospects of promotion by Clive and a possible crack at World Cup 2007. They all know the pecking order down to decimal points. They study form and know that the thirty-somethings out in New Zealand will not be around in three years. They remember how men like Chris Jones and James Simpson-Daniel made progress after their efforts here. I am going to select the strongest possible team, and if that means an inactive trip for some, well, that's pro rugby. The best available selection gives a better chance for the form players to thrive. To win is important, but the 80 minutes is not the be all and end all. The younger players will learn here and we will learn much about them by taking them away from their clubs and scrutinising them in a different environment. Can they fit in and adapt? After all, Test rugby is like driving on a motorway when you have been accustomed to poodling around the country lanes of the domestic scene.

'Canada and USA might not be among the leading nations, though Maori are advertised as being fifth in the world' – strange for a team whose selection is restricted – 'but all three hit hard and force defenders to make heavy hits. Being outside the top ten does not make them softer.'

With eerie prescience, Mallinder continued, 'If you relax for a second they can bang in a couple of tries in no time, undoing any previous good work.' Jim got that one right. In the semi-final – after Maori had amassed 69 points against USA – England were ambushed by hosts Canada in Calgary. A soothing 31-11 lead was abruptly transformed into a nastier-looking 31-23 scoreline, as Canada pounced for the couple of tries that Mallinder foresaw. England pulled away to win 48-23, with eight tries to three, including a pair for Dan Scarbrough and Jamie Noon. Vyvyan said: 'We were sloppy, the line out did not go well and we were disappointed to give away those tries. But we created some neat scores ourselves as we all try to make an impact.'

Some flaw in the manufacture of the shirts meant that anybody wearing a double figure (12, 13, 14, 15) had the second figure ripped off his back – except the left wing that is, who retained his two figure ones, that number seemingly having been attached with superglue. The two locks also lost their numbers. The effect was that five men were running round the pitch sporting No. 1. The man genuinely entitled to wear No. 1 – loose-head prop Mike Worsley – thought it was a marvellous idea. 'Anybody watching must have thought "that prop is a hard worker with great positional sense".'

But after the numbers fell off, so did the wheels when the circus moved 120 miles north to Edmonton's Commonwealth Stadium, which had recently staged the World Athletics Championships and could seat 63,000 – though less than 20,000 arrived for the day-long festivities, which included the finals of the women's tournament. Mallinder knew that the Maori would be a step up from Canada, especially in terms of confronting their ferocious tackling. 'Like having 15 Trevor Leotas coming at you' was his fearsome analogy. Four changes were made, plus Scarbrough going from wing to full back.

After conceding an early try, England aired some classy rugby but maddeningly with only one try to show for it. It was another beauty from Noon, with Dave Walder, Henry Paul and Mark Cueto all handling dextrously in the build-up. Still, five kicks from five by Walder contributed to a handy 19-5 half-time advantage. The Maori struck twice, in the 46th and 48th minutes, Paul's handling became loose, and

RIGHT Man of the future? England's Churchill Cup captain, Saracens-bound Hugh Vyvyan, on the ball against Canada.

the scores were locked at 19-19 throughout the rest of the second half and all through extra time, before Maori wing Hosea Gear ran 60 yards for the winner with seconds left.

It was an extra time too far in 78 degrees Fahrenheit for men who had slogged through since the previous August. It should have been different. Walder fired a penalty apparently clean through the posts, or where the posts would have been if they had not been stunted poles. That was in the 71st minute, but his kick was ruled out by the touch judges. English referee Dave Pearson told Walder that whatever he and Walder believed they had seen, the decision rested with the men standing by the posts. 'It looked OK to me and I told Dave so,' commented a bitter Walder.

So Maori won 26-19 and had the excuse to do another haka. Mallinder reflected: 'I liked the look of our back three,' which was Mike Horak, Cueto and Scarbrough against Canada, with Paul Sackey for Horak in the final. 'And Hugh is a fine captain. His leadership skills are evident and the squad respect him.' With England's main back row ageing, Vyvyan might be a man for the future, if he can tighten up his handling. Noon is a good bet to come through and improve England's midfield edge.

The Churchill Cup is scheduled to continue at least until 2007. 'It's a vital tournament for Canada and the US and especially for us now that we don't have the Six Nations A-team Championship in Europe any more. It's the main vehicle for us to view players on the way up' is Mallinder's view.

BEHIND SCOTTISH RUGBY.

Scotland in Samoa and Australia

by JILL DOUGLAS

'Only six Scots survived from the quarter-final showdown with the Wallabies in Brisbane, yet they took heart from a solid performance against Samoa …'

Scotland's tour Down Under achieved one important goal – it provided the side with its first Test victory in seven months, and the players with their first win under new coach Matt Williams. This was billed as a development tour and it certainly saw the emergence of some exciting new talent. But there is clearly some way to go before the Scots return to the kind of form that gave the Springboks a run for their money in Durban in the summer of 2003.

ABOVE Fly half Gordon Ross dives over for Scotland's first try in the 38-3 victory over Samoa in Wellington.

The personnel changes since the World Cup meant that the side named to play Samoa in the first international of the tour was dramatically different to the one that played in Australia last November. Yet nothing short of a convincing win would satisfy the Scots, who had won only three from their past twelve Tests and whose only other tour win came against the part-timers of NSW Country.

Injuries had depleted Williams's squad. The worst affected was the dynamic young centre Tom Philip, who suffered a freakish accident in training and returned home to undergo a full knee reconstruction. This allowed Williams to shuffle his deck and give Glasgow's player of the year, Sean

Lamont, his Test debut on the wing. Ben Hinshelwood came into the centre, and because of another injury to flanker Cameron Mather, Donnie Macfadyen won his third cap at open-side.

It was a wet and windswept Westpac Stadium in Wellington, chosen by Samoa as their home venue for this match. And the Pacific Islanders, now coached by the legendary All Black Michael Jones, were no walkover. They opened the scoring with a Roger Warren penalty and defended bravely for the opening quarter. But Scotland fly half Gordon Ross touched down just before the break – the first of five Scottish tries. Ben Hinshelwood, Ally Hogg, Simon Webster and replacement scrum half Mike Blair all added their names to the scoresheet in a 38-3 win. But the victory came at a price, since Chris Paterson had to remain in New Zealand for surgery on a badly broken cheekbone as the squad headed back to Australia for the first of two Tests against the Wallabies.

The Melbourne Test was to be Australia's first match since their World Cup final defeat to England in the autumn, and Eddie Jones had made four enforced changes, with Stirling Mortlock and Elton Flatley out injured. Clyde Rathbone made his debut at centre with Matt Giteau, and the Fijian-born Radike Samo started in the back row.

Only six Scots survived from the quarter-final showdown with the Wallabies in Brisbane, yet they took heart from a solid performance against Samoa and refused to be intimidated by the home side. This was a brave defensive display by the tourists, who trailed the Wallabies 13 points to 12 at the break thanks to four Dan Parks penalties. Joe Roff had kicked two and converted Matt Giteau's try to give Australia the lead.

Inevitably, however, the Wallabies' back three swung into action. Lote Tuqiri celebrated signing the largest contract in Australian rugby union history with two second-half tries, demonstrating why the Waratahs and the ARU were loath to see him return to league. And Wendell Sailor rounded off the evening's try count, gifted the ball when Simon Webster tried to chip over the wing's head. Sailor plucked it out of the air and raced in to secure the win. But the scoreline of 35-15 flattered the Wallabies, who were made to work hard by this Scotland team.

There were encouraging signs and an impressive debut start for full back Hugo Southwell. It was an afternoon of missed opportunities according to coach Matt Williams. 'I thought there were a lot of positives from our performance. I am just very disappointed about the last 14 points I think we gifted them after so much hard work. There are so many real positive things we can build on and the scoreline wasn't a reflection on the difference between the two teams.'

The Scots had only six days to regroup ahead of the second Test in Sydney's Telstra Stadium, and they were forced to spend much of that time speculating on what their second-row selection might be. Stuart Grimes was cited for stamping on Wallaby No. 8 David Lyons in the final minute of the game in Melbourne. Referee Paul Honiss had seen the incident and cautioned Grimes. However, he was handed a two-match ban by an IRB judicial committee and had his subsequent appeal turned down, despite receiving the support of the Wallabies' coach, Eddie Jones. With captain Scott Murray recovering from a hip injury, the loss of Grimes was a major blow to the Scots. A week of intensive treatment from the overworked Scotland medical team managed to put Murray on the pitch to partner Saracens-bound Iain Fullarton in the second row. Dan Parks, back in his home town, again received the nod at half back along with the impressive Chris Cusiter.

Again the Scots were made to ponder their missed chances, enjoying the lion's share of the possession; they looked good in defence but also staged attack after attack. For the first time under the new regime, this side strung together significant phases of play. Dan Parks kicked them into an early lead with a penalty, before Joe Roff levelled the scores. Then the forward power of this Australian side flexed its muscle with a scrum on Scotland's line. The resulting try was scored by Wendell Sailor, with Lote Tuqiri following up with another soon after. But the Scots battled back, and after Andy Henderson was denied his try when the referee was tackled by George Gregan, they powered over from the five-metre scrum. Chris Cusiter was the scorer; Parks added the conversion.

At 17-10 at half-time, the tourists were very much in this match, but there was always the suspicion that the enormously talented Australian back division would cut loose as they grew in confidence. Tuqiri crossed for his second; Morgan Turinui and the ubiquitous Joe Roff also breached the Scotland line to give a final score of 34-13 in the Wallabies' favour.

Yet overall, some encouraging signs came from this inexperienced Scotland team, and there was the opportunity for Craig Hamilton and Graeme Morrison to gain their first taste of Test match rugby. Matt Williams again felt the final tally was not a fair return for the endeavors of his young team. 'I am very disappointed with that final scoreline. I believe we played better than that. It doesn't reflect the difference between the sides. I thought our game plan was good and our guys executed it with great passion and precision. When we got to within five metres of the Wallabies' try line, we made some basic errors, a bit of white-line fever.'

That fever cost them dearly in the end, with the Wallabies wrapping up the Hopetoun Cup with two straight victories. It is 22 years since Scotland beat Australia, and it was always a long shot to imagine they would redress that record on this tour.

Wales in Argentina and South Africa   by GRAHAM CLUTTON

'The first half ... saw them play the best rugby of the trip, with Shane Williams scoring three tries, including one sidestepping work of genius, as they built up a 25-0 interval lead.'

O n the face of it, the facts and figures from Mike Ruddock's first tour as Wales coach don't make for great reading. The three-week excursion to Argentina and South Africa produced just one victory from three matches, with Ruddock's men conceding 123 points and 16 tries along the way. It was certainly not what the doctor had ordered. Having said all of that, there are plenty of other statistics which are equally valid when putting the ill-timed trip into context. To start with, the tour came at the end of a gruelling 11-month season during which Wales had already played 15 matches. They also had to travel to two different continents and two different time zones – and they did so without a full team of internationals due to a horrendous injury list.

Fatigue and the normal end-of-season problems deprived Ruddock of key men like Gareth Thomas, Stephen Jones, Robin McBryde, Gareth Cooper and the soon to be Bradford-bound Iestyn

Harris. On top of that, Ruddock and fitness adviser Andrew Hore decided to leave at home the former captain Martyn Williams, who, in their eyes, needed a summer in the gymnasium to bulk up.

The consequence of having all these high-profile absentees was that Wales flew out to Argentina with a relatively inexperienced squad that featured a significant number of international novices. And as Ruddock knew from his past experience in South America, it was unlikely to be a straightforward trip to take on the Pumas. That being the case, what they badly needed was a smooth, incident-free passage into the first Test in Tucuman.

Some hope of that. After all, this is Wales on tour we are talking about – the Wales that were a day late leaving for their Australasian trip in the summer of 2003 because of a pay dispute. Money matters were to prove the problem again this time, with the storm brewing up around skipper Colin Charvis, who claimed he was, once again, being short-changed by the governing body.

His gripe concerned his loss of earnings from having left French club Tarbes early to link up with the Welsh squad, and in order to make a point over this compensation issue he refused to speak to the press at one media session. Not too many would have complained about that considering his strained relationship with the media. However, it was hardly what Ruddock wanted to hear when approached by the disgruntled press pack.

Charvis's decision to ignore all was the cue for all hell to break loose back home, with former Wales captains calling for the controversial

LEFT Half of Wales descends on Fourie du Preez during the Test against South Africa in Pretoria.

BELOW Shane Williams's dancing feet take him to the Argentinian line for the second of three tries in Buenos Aires.

PAGE 80 Tour success Dwayne Peel whips the ball away while another, Adam Jones, keeps the Pumas at bay.

player to be stripped of the captaincy and sent home, while his actions went down like a lead balloon with the WRU bigwigs. The man you really felt sorry for was Ruddock, as it was the last thing he needed to be dealing with just 48 hours before his first Test as Wales coach.

That game ended in a 50-44 defeat to Argentina amid the crumbling concrete and barbed wire of Tucuman, and, almost inevitably, Charvis was to prove the villain of the piece, with his first-half sin-binning a pivotal moment. Up to that point, Wales had had the upper hand, but his dismissal was followed immediately by the first try of the game from opposing skipper Gonzalo Longo. A further burst of three Puma touchdowns inside the opening six minutes of the second half left the visitors with too steep a mountain to climb, despite a thrilling late rally.

Morale was hardly helped by a stomach bug that swept through the Welsh camp, but, to their credit, Ruddock's men put their troubles to one side to level the series with a 35-20 win in Buenos Aires. The first half of that match saw them play the best rugby of the trip, with Shane Williams scoring three tries, including one sidestepping work of genius, as they built up a 25-0 interval lead. What was equally impressive was the character they showed in holding on in the face of a Pumas fightback after the break, with fly half Nicky Robinson sealing the win by rounding off a superbly worked try.

So it was off to South Africa in good spirits. But, in the end, up against a powerful and pacy Bokke outfit, Wales found this eighteenth match of the season to be a game too far. Losing key forwards Brent Cockbain and Michael Owen in the week leading up to the Test hardly helped, nor did the further injury-enforced exits of Deiniol Jones, Nicky Robinson and Alix Popham during the course of the match. By the end of the game, Wales were held together with sticky tape, with the hamstrung Charvis playing on one leg and reserve hooker Huw Bennett packing down on the blind-side flank. However, it has to be said they didn't help their cause with some pretty shoddy defence, as they leaked seven tries during a 53-18 defeat. That had also been a major issue in the first Test in Argentina, in which, if anything, it had been more painful, as that was a game Wales could – and probably should – have won.

Ruddock was quick to stress that the number of tries conceded on tour was down to individual errors rather than to a failure of the new rush-defence system, but whatever the reasons, he'll want to shore things up for next season, while also acquiring more composure in attack. However, he will have been encouraged by individual plusses to come out of the tour, with Robinson and Gavin Henson impressing in Argentina, Adam Jones taking big strides on the most daunting of tours for a young prop, Huw Bennett coming of age and Michael Owen making a smooth transition to No. 8, with scrum half Dwayne Peel perhaps emerging as the player of the trip.

Ruddock will also be looking forward to receiving quality reinforcements come the autumn, when we will be able to make a fuller assessment of his coaching credentials at this level.

Ireland in South Africa

by SEAN DIFFLEY

'There had been stories circulating that there was a certain amount of dissension in the Springbok camp, but there were no signs of anything like that when the games began.'

Just like the World War II slogan 'Is your journey really necessary?', for the Irish squad, with the triple crown under its belt and a victory over world champions England among the season's household gods, the two-Test series in South Africa appeared a step or two too far. In addition a controversy developed just before the journey about bonus payments and match fees. There were suggestions that the players might even have recourse to a strike and refuse to go to South Africa. And that raised the possibility that the Irish Rugby Football Union would have been faced with all sorts of difficulties, not least the financial loss such an eventuality would entail for the South Africans.

However, the situation was resolved and the team flew out to Cape Town. Many felt that the whole pre-tour spot of bother was merely a spate of megaphone-style negotiation that really should have been taken care of behind closed doors. It didn't impress the Irish rugby public, conscious that the very well-paid players were already costing the game a huge amount in a country with small rugby-playing resources. But the matter was fairly quickly forgotten, and although Ireland lost both Tests, in Bloemfontein and Cape Town, they did, overall, perform better than the other northern hemisphere adventurers – England, Scotland and Wales.

There had been stories circulating that there was a certain amount of dissension in the Springbok camp, but there were no signs of anything like that when the games began. The South Africans, on the contrary, revealed that they are very likely to become a force to be reckoned with, with a lively young side displaying skill and, above all, tremendous physical power as they dominated possession in the first Test, which they won 31-17.

Ireland were very disappointing in that Test, played at altitude in Bloemfontein. The line out, which had so impressed in the Six Nations with Paul O'Connell and Malcolm O'Kelly so effective, was nowhere near as efficient, and Ronan O'Gara kicked away far too much possession. This virtually handed

ABOVE Brian O'Driscoll steps on the gas as he makes one of his signature breaks through the South African defence in the first Test in Bloemfontein.

RIGHT Paul O'Connell so nearly scores for Ireland in Cape Town.

PAGE 81 Springbok second-row Bakkies Botha, both a line-out force and a double try scorer in the Bloemfontein Test, soars above the Irish challenge.

the ball back to the Springboks, for whom Bakkies Botha was the principal force out of touch. And it was Botha, after a mere four minutes, who ambled over for a try for South Africa.

Then – and it didn't happen with any great frequency – the Irish managed a back movement, with Brian O'Driscoll carving his way in typical style through the middle to send wing Shane Horgan over for a try. A couple of O'Gara penalty goals and two from South African full back Gaffie du Toit had the teams level, 11-11, at half-time.

Gordon D'Arcy's departure after half an hour with a groin injury – he was replaced as O'Driscoll's centre partner by Kevin Maggs – had been a blow, but with 20 minutes to go the Irish were only 17-21 behind. But they were unable to catch up. O'Gara had kicked two more penalties, but a try from centre Wayne Julies, a second from Botha and a bizarre score from back-row Pedrie Wannenburg sealed Ireland's fate. Ireland, at touch near their left corner flag, called a short line out, and the usually reliable hooker, Shane Byrne, threw the ball directly to an unmarked Wannenburg, who dropped over the line unchallenged.

The Irish had flown from their base in Cape Town to altitude for that first Test just two days before the game. Was that a big mistake? Was that the reason for the rather listless Irish performance? It was denied of course, but the fact is that it was an entirely different display by Ireland a week later at the sea-level Newlands in Cape Town.

Ireland began well in Cape Town. A vigilant O'Driscoll lobbed a high but very accurate pass to the left after just seven minutes, and wing Tyrone Howe got in for his try. O'Gara converted and so Ireland led 7-0. But by half-time the Springboks were 20-10 ahead, with tries coming from wings Breyton Paulse and Jaque Fourie.

Nevertheless South Africa were not allowed to stroll home as happened at Bloemfontein. David Humphreys replaced a clearly out-of-form O'Gara at out-half and he certainly galvanized the Irish. With about 15 minutes to go he put in a crafty kick over the South African line, and O'Driscoll, lurking at his shoulder, was on to the ball like a flash for an excellent try that Humphreys converted. Indeed in the last 20 minutes of the match the Irish troubled the Springboks, who began to lose their composure a bit. Following O'Driscoll's try, the score stood at 23-17 for South Africa with a now rampant Ireland just a converted try short of a win. Instead the Springboks raised the siege, and Ireland, in injury time, conceded a penalty that Percy Montgomery, who had an excellent all-round game, slotted over for three points and a 26-17 victory. Ireland have yet to win a Test in South Africa.

Jake White, the South Africa coach, put the series in perspective. 'In our country we have been gifted by generations of big players. As the great Doc Craven said once, a good big one will always beat a good little one. A country like Ireland will always have the numbers against them. In South Africa we are blessed to have big players. When you see somebody like prop Os du Randt making a tackle on an out-half after 76 minutes, you know that in the modern game, rather than forwards and backs, you need 15 athletes.'

Indeed, but even professional athletes need an off season. In the old amateur days there was a four-month break. Now it's less than one month. The shenanigans south of the equator this summer didn't necessarily mean that after England's World Cup triumph the power has swung back towards the Tri-Nations. It all just illustrates that certain teams were tired out from a long home season. It's a general problem the IRB must get to grips with.

HOME FRONT

Duckworth's Dream
Worcester in the Premiership
by ALASTAIR HIGNELL

"'I am very emotional," he said, "because this is the culmination of over ten years of hard work. We have made our mistakes in the past, and had the disappointment of previous seasons' defeats ... but we've learnt from our mistakes and moved forward. We've come a long way.'"

Worcester won 26 matches out of 26 to win the first division title by 17 points. Rotherham lost 22 matches out of 22 and finished bottom of the Premiership by a massive 34 points. The decision for the one to replace the other in rugby's top flight should have been rubber-stamped in less time than it takes to get to the end of this sentence. But there's an easy way and an ERL way. For the third successive season a straightforward rugby issue was clouded by off-field considerations involving ground capacity and planning regulations. This time it was made even more ugly because the clubs involved had history.

Two years before, Rotherham had beaten Worcester to the first division title, only to be told that their Clifton Lane ground didn't meet the criteria laid down for clubs in the Zurich Premiership by England Rugby Limited. Worcester owner Cecil Duckworth believed that his Rotherham counterpart, Mike Yarlett, had acquiesced too readily in the decision. Subsequent allegations of a financial arrangement between Rotherham and the existing Premiership clubs gave rise to both the

ABOVE Cecil Duckworth of Worcester. 'When I first came to the club, the view was that it would take ten years to get to the top. I had hoped to get there sooner, but after all the disappointments, I'm glad we've arrived.'

LEFT Worcester's Chris Garrard scores in the promotion-clinching 68-15 win over Bristol.

PAGE 88 Worcester director of rugby John Brain.

Arlidge inquiry and bitter blood between the two clubs. Rotherham beat Worcester twice on the field to clinch promotion the season before last, but even though heading in the opposite direction this time around couldn't resist the chance to rain on Worcester's parade.

Even though the RFU professed themselves happy with Worcester's plans to increase their Sixways ground capacity to meet Premiership requirements, Rotherham threw in a legal challenge over the timing of the application. It took England Rugby Limited a week's consultation with their own lawyers before rugby justice could be served.

However frustrating it might have been in the short term, Worcester Warriors fans should have taken an extra seven days on tenterhooks in their stride. This was, after all, the sixth consecutive season that they had had promotion in their grasp. Rotherham had beaten them three times to the first division title, while Bristol and Leeds had also forced them into second place. This time around the Warriors bowed to no one. From the first match of the season (a 26-20 win at Otley) to the last (a 49-31 victory over near neighbours Pertemps Bees) Worcester crushed all opposition. In the process they beat nearest rivals Orrell 40-14 at home and 15-7 away, scored 1,119 points in conceding just 339 and clinched the title with three matches to spare with a 68-15 win at home to Bristol.

For Duckworth, too, the overriding emotion was one of relief. The multimillionaire got involved soon after selling Worcester Heat Systems to Bosch in 1992, when Worcester were close to the lowest point in their history. In 1988-89 Worcester had been relegated to North Midlands Division One. With Duckworth's backing, they gained seven promotions in ten seasons before earning themselves the unenviable reputation as the 'nearly men' of division one. Not before time, the unassuming Duckworth could crack the champagne.

'I am very emotional,' he said, 'because this is the culmination of over ten years of hard work. We have made our mistakes in the past, and had the disappointment of previous seasons' defeats at Headingley, Clifton Lane and Millmoor, but we've learnt from our mistakes and moved forward. We've come a long way.'

Many of those mistakes arose from a bizarre recruiting policy, which had earned Worcester and their owner the reputation as increasingly desperate big spenders with more money than sense. In four frantic seasons the Warriors got through four coaches and over a hundred players. Ben Clarke and David Pears of England, Craig Chalmers and Cameron Mather of Scotland, Kingsley Jones from Wales, Alistair Murdoch of Australia, Werner Swanepoel of South Africa – all came and went through the revolving doors at Sixways, closely accompanied by the likes of Earl Va'a and Sililo Martens. Les

Cusworth and Geoff Cooke briefly held the coaching reins, as did Phil Maynard and Adrian Skeggs. And the more elusive the holy grail of Premiership rugby, the more frenetic the signings, the more frequent the rumours that Duckworth was about to pull the plug.

The arrival of the unheralded John Brain as director of rugby in 2001 and his recruitment of Andy Keast as head coach a year later came just in time. The former Gloucester lock and the ex-policeman brought focus and hard work to Sixways. It took two seasons to weed out the less committed and two seasons to get the playing structure right. 'We targeted players who were talented but were also prepared to work hard,' commented Brain. 'They had to be interested in putting the team first.'

The Warriors' perfect record on the pitch last season was, for Duckworth, the final validation of all his efforts off it. 'When I first came to the club, the view was that it would take ten years to get to the top. I had hoped to get there sooner, but after all the disappointments, I'm glad we've arrived. What I wanted to create was something that was lasting and of value to the community. I think we have fostered an appetite for rugby in the city. When I was first here, there were 50 people watching. Now there are 5,000. However, in my mind, if we hadn't got Worcester to the Premiership, I would have failed. We would have come a long way, but we would not have met our objectives. That was why this season was so important, and we've got everything right.'

And Duckworth believes that the late drama brought the best out of an already close group at Worcester. 'It was a particularly difficult time for the players and coaches,' he said. 'When there was so much uncertainty it would have been easy to point fingers, but they never did. We all stuck together, kept faith and we've come through it. It has made us an even stronger unit. Rotherham's actions were disgraceful but we can now enjoy the moment and look forward to the future.'

John Brain agrees. 'Our preparation has not really been affected by this situation but personally it has been very frustrating. These last seven days, we have felt like we were on trial. As a result, I think we are even more determined to make an impression next season.'

The stakes are high, but the ambitions at Sixways are lofty. As far as Brain is concerned, 'I have already put promotion in the cupboard. The next big thing that needs to be done is to keep Worcester in the Premiership.' And that is just the start. 'The coaching staff and the players have delivered the dream for Cecil Duckworth. But that's only a part of it, because we know he wants Worcester to be a top team not just in England, but also in Europe.'

But Brain knows that history and the odds are stacked against Worcester. Rotherham have twice bounced straight back into the first division after leaving barely a mark on the top flight. Leeds would have been relegated at the end of their first season in the Premiership if promotion had not been barred to Rotherham. Bristol came up on the back of Malcolm Pearce's big-money investment but fell from grace as he started to feel the financial pinch.

Duckworth has deeper pockets than the latter and greater resources than the former. 'Rotherham's experience in the Premiership was dismal,' he admits, 'but we are such a different club. We have better facilities, better support, a better squad and in John Brain and Andy Keast, two coaches who know what is required in the top flight. That makes us a totally different proposition.'

Not surprisingly, therefore, optimism was unbounded at the start of the new season. The new East Stand – raising the capacity by 4,000 – was fast taking shape. So was a new squad. French international wing Thomas Lombard had signed from Stade Français, while England international Pat Sanderson had joined from Harlequins, and Springbok Thinus Delport had moved down the road from Gloucester. England Under 21 scrum half Clive Stuart-Smith was on his way from Leeds, and prop Chris Horsman from London Irish. Wallaby outside half Stephen Larkham was tempted before deciding to stay put in Canberra. Compatriot Matthew Burke in the end opted for Newcastle.

And the fixture planners at ERL also seemed intent on making up for their colleagues on the board of management, as they gave Worcester an opening-day fixture at home – against a Newcastle side expecting to welcome Jonny Wilkinson back to competitive rugby – and lobbed home fixtures against Bath, Gloucester and Parker Pen Challenge Cup holders Harlequins into the autumn schedule at Sixways for good measure.

Have the Warriors got what it takes to stay in the top flight? Can they make a decent fist of Premiership rugby or will they find that like arch-rivals Rotherham they are out of their depth? We'll all know soon enough.

Bath Denied the 2003-04 Zurich Championship
by CHRIS HEWETT

'The first hint that the title would remain in the hands of Lawrence Dallaglio, Rob Howley and company was dropped, ironically enough, at Bath in the first week of February.'

The good folk of Gloucester, earthy and unforgiving in equal measure, have never had much time for their near neighbours from Bath, whom they consider too precious by half. So when the Recreation Grounders, league leaders for virtually the whole of the regular campaign, knocked seven bells out of the Cherry and Whites in the final game of the 22-match programme to guarantee themselves a place in the Zurich Premiership final at Twickenham, a chastened sct of Kingsholmites easily resisted the temptation to offer their formal congratulations. Instead, they took huge delight in reminding Bath that their considerable achievements over the previous nine months counted for precisely nothing in terms of actually winning the trophy.

Of course, Gloucester had first-hand experience of this apparent contradiction. The previous year, they had topped the table by 15 points after winning four games more than any of their rivals, only to lose 39-3 to a fit, perfectly prepared and highly motivated Wasps team in the final. Much was made of the injustice of it all; critics of the system highlighted the fact that Wasps played two meaningful matches in the run-up to Twickenham while Gloucester were confined in a straitjacket of enforced inactivity. And here were Bath, much to the delight of their West Country cousins, in precisely the same boat.

Precisely? Maybe not quite. Bath certainly found themselves at a disadvantage in terms of preparation – having failed to arrange meaningful fixtures in France and Wales, their only means of filling the long weeks of doing nothing much was to play a semi-competitive match at Newbury a few days before the final. Wasps, meanwhile, could scarcely have been more competitive in terms of their interim fixtures. First, they had to qualify for the final by beating Northampton at the Causeway Stadium. Then there was the small matter of a Heineken Cup final against Toulouse, who stretched the Londoners to snapping point before self-destructing in the last few seconds.

As in 2003, so in 2004 – the table-toppers undercooked; Wasps in a state of optimum readiness for the struggle. Yet there were subtle differences, for Bath had not dominated the league programme in the way Gloucester had the previous season. While Gloucester, with Ludovic Mercier and Olivier Azam in their pomp, had scored far more heavily than any of their rivals, Bath's claims to supremacy were based squarely on the most determined defence since Davy Crockett spent 13 quality days at the Alamo. What was more, Wasps signalled their grasping intentions far earlier on this occasion. They looked so dangerous from Christmas onwards that there was an ominous predictability as to how the campaign would be resolved.

The first hint that the title would remain in the hands of Lawrence Dallaglio, Rob Howley and company was dropped, ironically enough, at Bath in the first week of February. Wasps, armed with a sensational young open-side flanker by the name of Jonny O'Connor and an aggressive defensive system that broke hearts as well as ribs, pinched a narrow victory on the banks of the Avon in a game of exceptional physicality. As Bath had been watertight on their own territory all season, this was a result full of significance.

If the West Countrymen were not quite devastated by the setback, it was because they were happy to be performing above the expectations of everyone – Jack Rowell, John Connolly, Michael Foley, Danny Grewcock, you name them.

The previous May, they had found themselves a single defeat away from relegation and a probable merger with Bristol that would effectively have stripped them of an identity forged in almost 140 years of thud and blunder amid the Roman ruins and Georgian splendour. Now, they were punching their weight once again, having recruited with intelligence during the close season.

Recruit number one was Connolly himself – dear old 'Knuckles', the Australian with a face like a dried peach, who had worked with Queensland and the Wallabies, with Stade Français and Swansea. One

BELOW Centre Stuart Abbott beats the Bath cover to score Wasps' try in the final.

of the game's most celebrated thinkers and strategists, he arrived from West Wales with a brief to head up the hands-on operation, thereby allowing Rowell to contribute a white-collared overview from the director of rugby's office and Foley, a long-time protégé from Brisbane days, to concentrate on the nuts and bolts of coaching. There were other Australians on the staff, most notably Richard Graham and Brian Smith, both of whom made handsome contributions to the renaissance. But it was Connolly who provided the inspiration.

There were also some striking additions to the playing squad. Bath picked up the likes of Michael Lipman, Andrew Higgins and Lee Best from Bristol, who had contrived to pip their nearest and dearest to bottom spot in 2003 and had seen their professional squad evaporate as a result. They also moved for Isaac Fea'unati, the ball-carrying Samoan No. 8 who had completed tours of Premiership duty with both London Irish and Leeds, and Martyn Wood, who left Wasps when it became clear that Howley would have his pick of the big games. Rob Fidler pitched up from Gloucester, while Robbie Fleck arrived from South Africa, having called time on his Springbok career. And already materialised from the same part of the world, the young Matt Stevens was a prop forward built like a medium-sized wildebeest and blessed with the handling skills of an inside centre.

Yet in many ways, two of Stevens's fellow members of the propping fraternity were responsible for transforming Bath's fortunes in the world's most demanding, least forgiving club league. David Flatman, a close friend of Grewcock's, finally agreed terms after a long courtship and moved from Saracens, bringing with him his iron strength and impeccable loose-head technique. He gave the Bath pack the most solid of platforms from which to build a back-to-the-future game constructed around the forward power of yesteryear, when the Chilcotts and Dawes and Redmans and Halls were clad in the blue, black and white. Alongside him appeared the mountainous Duncan Bell, cast aside by England after the 1998 'tour from hell' but revered as a local hero by the knowledgeable townsmen of Pontypridd, where he earned his corn before recrossing the Severn Bridge.

Remarkably, Bath fielded the same starting pack – Flatman and Bell propping Jonathan Humphreys; Fidler and the outstanding line-out burglar Steve Borthwick in the second row; Andy Beattie, Lipman and Fea'unati in the back row – throughout the first half of the campaign, and changed it only when Grewcock returned from World Cup business in Australia. The continuity at forward compensated for a veritable *Emergency – Ward 10* situation among the backs, who seemed to break down for a pastime. There were courageous victories at Wasps, at Leicester, at Gloucester. Utterly secure at the scrummage, supreme at the line out – Mark Evans, the Harlequins coach, described this part of Bath's act as a 'Rolls-Royce job' – and able to bank on the cool-headedness, durability and accurate goal-kicking of Olly Barkley, they developed a collective fortitude that proved fiendishly difficult to overcome.

They qualified for the 2004-05 Heineken Cup, always the primary target for these European pioneers, well before the end of the season, which may partially explain why their form diminished in mid-spring. Injuries were another factor – if Fleck and Mike Catt happened to be fit, Iain Balshaw and Matt Perry would inevitably be crook. In successive weeks, Bath lost a Premiership game at Northampton and messed up a Parker Pen Challenge Cup semi-final against Montferrand before throwing away a winning lead at Harlequins. Suddenly, they had to beat Gloucester to deprive Wasps, who looked scarcely beatable at this point, of top spot.

And beat them they did, in flabbergasting fashion. Having spent the season preventing opposition tries rather than scoring their own, Bath cut loose before the usual sell-out crowd at the Rec and won 41-7, with five-pointers from Beattie, the blind-side flanker who had forced his way into the representative reckoning with some ruthlessly muscular performances, and three of the club's less familiar players – reserve hooker Lee Mears, South African wing Wylie Human and home-grown centre Alex Crockett. Chris Malone, another southern hemisphere type, did the rest with his right boot, and did it so well that Barkley, a little out of form and a lot out of favour, remained a bit-part actor for the remainder of the programme.

Bath knew full well they would not score four tries against Wasps – not with the Londoners operating their 'up and in' defence with increasing efficiency. So they developed a strategy for the final that could hardly have been less extravagant. They assumed that their front row would boss the set pieces, even though the influential Flatman was out of the picture with an injury to his heel, and that Borthwick and his fellow jumpers would slaughter the reigning champions at the line out. Armed with a surfeit of possession, they would attack in the narrowest of channels, throwing everything bar the kitchen sink at Howley and Alex King in an attempt to sever Wasps' line of communication. If Bath's outside backs were to be used at all, it would be in a water-carrying role.

So unambitious an approach did not deserve to work, but it very nearly hit the jackpot. In a first half full of brutal exchanges between the forwards – Paul Volley, the tough-nut Wasps flanker, was kicked to high heaven and back after landing on the wrong side of a ruck – Borthwick decimated the champions' line out, repeatedly competing for Trevor Leota's wayward deliveries and dominating the aerial battle. The challengers secured great swathes of territory and almost limitless possession, allowing Beattie and Fea'unati to make big yardages with ball in hand. Yet Bath, a team wholly without width, never once looked like scoring a try. All they had to show for their sweat-bucket efforts in the first 40 minutes was a single, miserable penalty from Malone.

When the interval whistle sounded, Wasps jogged off together, with the air of a team who knew they had absorbed the worst that could be inflicted upon them. What was more, they suspected that one breakaway try would be enough to earn another year's custody of the Premiership trophy. Sure enough, that try arrived early in the second half. Grewcock, almost as effective a line-out forward as Borthwick, provided yet more clean ball for Bath, who were in perfect shape to launch another of their claustrophobic assaults. But when Malone received a crisp pass from Wood, he received the rapacious Volley at the same time. The ball went loose, Tom Voyce hoovered it up – how Bath must now regret losing the wing to Wasps – and flicked it on to the unmarked Stuart Abbott, who was far too rapid for the covering defenders.

As the only other scores were a dropped goal apiece for the two outside halves, Wasps prevailed 10-6 – a mirror image of the score at the Rec three and a half months earlier. The Londoners openly admitted that Bath had made them dig deep in the bump-and-grind areas of the game, but they also pointed out that if they were to be beaten on an occasion as grand as this one, it would not be by a side incapable of playing anything more challenging than ten-man rugby.

To a man and woman, the Bath supporters understood and accepted this sporting truth. There were no cries of 'we wuz robbed'; there were not even any bleats about the iniquities of a system that failed to reward a team for finishing top of the heap after 22 games against all and sundry. Instead, they pronounced themselves grateful for the ride – a more pleasant trip, certainly, than the one they had endured in 2002-03 – and acknowledged Wasps as the more rounded, more flexible and more gifted side. Defeat has never been a popular form of entertainment at the Recreation Ground, but given where the local boys had started from the previous September, it was just about tolerable here. Just this once, mind you.

The Falcons Strike the 2004 Powergen Cup Final
by ALASTAIR HIGNELL

'But then came the Vyvyan charge-down, the Dowson try and the Walder conversion to … ensure a second cup victory for the Falcons and a second heartache for the Sharks.'

As a player, Newcastle Falcons' director of rugby Rob Andrew gained a not always deserved reputation as being cautious, pragmatic and safe. In winning a thrilling Powergen Cup final, his team were anything but. Newcastle outscored attack-orientated Sale Sharks by four tries to three and came from behind five times to win the highest-scoring cup final ever. The winning try, scored five minutes from the end of normal time by replacement forward Phil Dowson, earned the Falcons their second knockout title in four years and salvaged an otherwise indifferent season for the Northeasterners.

The Falcons won only seven Zurich Premiership matches all year and finished fourth from bottom in the league, but the four victories they gained in the cup were enough to secure them a coveted and potentially lucrative place in Europe's premier club competition, the Heineken Cup.

Sale apart, their only other real test came in the quarter-finals, when London Irish came to Kingston Park on the back of a sixth-round victory at Gloucester and lost 24-12. Otherwise, the Falcons were barely stretched in beating Rotherham 38-10 at Millmoor in the sixth round, while their semi-final against part-timers Pertemps Bees was a 53-3 romp.

Sale's passage to the final was altogether tougher. After a thrilling 43-28 sixth-round victory against Leicester at Welford Road, the Sharks crushed Saracens 26-3 at Edgeley Park in the quarter-finals and outgunned Leeds 33-20 in the semis. Their Premiership form may have been just as patchy as their opponents', but they arrived at Twickenham with a determination to play fast, loose and to their strengths out wide, where the back three of Jason Robinson, Steve Hanley and Mark Cueto were in prolific form. In the extraordinarily athletic Chris Jones, whose enormous potential had already been recognised with an England debut, and their miniature but mobile hooker Andy Titterell, the Sharks had forwards expected to revel in Twickenham's wide open spaces.

Newcastle were without World Cup winner Jonny Wilkinson and, despite boasting their own exciting England-qualified backs in the shapes of Jamie Noon and wings Michael Stephenson and Tom May, were expected, by contrast, to keep it tighter, relying on Wilkinson's understudy Dave Walder to control operations behind a heavier pack, in which international locks Stuart Grimes and Garath Archer provided the grunt and props Micky Ward and Ian Peel the growl. That theory was exploded from the kick-off.

In perfect conditions, the Falcons launched a series of exhilarating and expansive attacks that initially had Sale clutching at shadows. They

LEFT Newcastle full back Joe Shaw's aerobatics signal the Falcons' third try of the final.

BELOW Jason Robinson on the attack for the Sharks.

PAGES 98-99 Phil Dowson touches down the winning score despite desperate Sale defence.

had their first try on the board after just seven minutes, when South African flanker Warren Britz crossed from close range after an offload from centre Mark Mayerhofler, with Walder converting to open up a 7-0 lead.

Sale, however, soon put a nightmare start behind them and started playing to their principles. Outside half Charlie Hodgson, feeling his way back to form and fitness after a lengthy injury, banged over a penalty, converted a scintillating try by Hanley on the left wing, and then exchanged penalties with Walder to keep the Sharks ahead at the interval.

Cue the captain. Saracens-bound Newcastle No. 8 Hugh Vyvyan marked his last major game in a Falcons shirt with a commanding second-half performance. Within minutes of it starting, he had powered over for his team's second try. Within minutes of it ending he had created the winning score for Dowson. No wonder that at the end of an extended lap of honour, he owned up to mixed emotions. 'It's unbelievable. It was a great effort from the boys. We kept coming back at them and I was so proud to be part of it. At this moment it does seem bizarre to be leaving the club, and that's why it was a very emotional moment for me to be lifting the cup.'

Between touching down at the start of the second period and hoisting high the silverware, Vyvyan and his Newcastle team had a helter-skelter to ride. Moments after Walder converted his captain's score, Newcastle were behind again. Swift handling from the Sharks backs created space for Cueto on the left and the England tourist showed just why he is so highly rated with a superb individual try, first going round Tom May on the outside before slicing through the cover defence to score under the posts. Hodgson converted, and added another penalty.

Both sides were by now playing high-risk rugby. It has never been in Sale's nature to try to sit on a lead, while Newcastle were happy to enter into the spirit of the occasion. A series of lightning raids down the left created a try up the middle for full back Joe Shaw, who ran on to a short pass from Walder after the outside half had looped Mayerhofler in midfield. Shaw's extravagant touchdown, in which he swallow-dived several feet into the air before scoring, may have caused some physical damage to the player but as an expression of the joyous nature of the spectacle, it was entirely fitting.

Not to be outdone, Sale scored almost immediately, centre Chris Mayor racing over after another bout of bewildering running and passing from the Sharks backs. Sale were back in front and the clock was ticking down. If the final whistle had blown then, few in the 48,000 crowd would have asked for their money back. Sharks coach Jim Mallinder, captain on the only other occasion Sale had played in a cup final – losing to Leicester in 1996 – would have been overjoyed. He would have been just as happy if full-time had been blown a few minutes later, when after the agony of seeing Walder level the scores with a couple of penalties came the ecstasy of an even later and potentially match-winning penalty from Hodgson.

But then came the Vyvyan charge-down, the Dowson try and the Walder conversion to bring the final scoreline to 37-33 and ensure a second cup victory for the Falcons and a second heartache for the Sharks. Mallinder as ever was gracious in a defeat that would cost his team a place in the European elite. 'There were two very similar sides out there, playing good attacking rugby. We had a couple of opportunities to make the game safe, but we didn't take them. We were a bit naive at times, and didn't get out of our half when we should have done. That cost us.'

His captain, the hugely competitive and hugely committed Peter Anglesea, was less philosophical. 'To be quite honest,' he told the post-match briefing, 'defeat today felt like a death in the family.'

Winning director of rugby Rob Andrew was, by contrast, all smiles. 'At least we were in front when the music stopped,' he joked before going on to applaud the approach of both teams. 'It was a brilliant final. Our players were magnificent, and so were Sale's. Being in the Heineken Cup next year is a big bonus.'

Qualification for Europe is, of course, a huge carrot dangling in front of the cup winners, and Newcastle snatched hungrily at it. The incentive has been one of the salvations of an otherwise threatened competition. There is a line of thinking that suggests that in an increasingly crowded season, with top players at risk from burn-out due to the ever-growing demands of a high-impact collision sport, the one expendable tournament is the Powergen Cup. The rationale put forward to sustain that argument has always been that rugby as a sport rarely throws up any shocks and that the cup as a competition rarely throws up any surprises.

Powergen 2003-04 quite thrillingly exploded that argument. The sixth round saw the early exit of two of the greatest names in cup history. Holders Gloucester were humbled at home by London Irish, while Leicester were savaged in front of their own fans by Sale. In the quarters, record winners Bath bowed out and so did last year's finalists Northampton, while Wasps, current Premiership champions, on their way to a Heineken-Zurich double, were dumped on their backsides by Pertemps Bees, a team with the temerity to come not just from outside the elite, but from outside the Premiership.

Then came the final, a showcase that lived up to and then exceeded its billing. The highest-scoring final in the history of the competition was also the best in living memory. Newcastle just about deserved their victory and their place next year in Europe. The Powergen Cup itself removed any doubts about its place in the rugby calendar.

Wasps Bring Home the Big One
the 2003-04 Heineken Cup

by **CHRIS JONES**

'The massive high created by the Dublin heroics was undermined by successive Zurich defeats by Gloucester and Leicester, and it was with much trepidation that Wasps fans headed to Twickenham. After all, Toulouse were the Manchester United of European rugby ...'

It epitomised the London Wasps work ethic that had allowed the players to defeat holders Toulouse 27-20 at Twickenham and claim the ultimate European rugby prize – the Heineken Cup. As Warren Gatland, the Wasps director of rugby, tried to take in the enormity of the achievement he had plotted, he couldn't help thinking ahead to the Zurich Premiership play-off final against Bath that Wasps faced the following weekend – also at HQ.

Gatland said: 'There is no point being champions of Europe if you are not going to be champions of England.' They ended the season with both titles, and even the former All Black hooker could then take time off from goal setting to savour a job well done.

It will come as no surprise to anyone who has spent a nanosecond with the Wasps players and management to discover that they all share Gatland's desire for even greater success. Gatland

LEFT Rob Howley pounces for the winning try in the Heineken Cup final at Twickenham, leaving a disconsolate Clément Poitrenaud in his wake.

RIGHT Bigger, stronger, more confident – Wasps wing Tom Voyce in action in the Heineken quarter-final against Gloucester.

has a kindred spirit in club captain Lawrence Dallaglio, who has now become a World Cup winner and European champion as well as leader of the English club champions yet again. While many players would be happy with that rugby CV, Dallaglio is eager to build on this success. He wants to emulate Leicester, who won back-to-back Heineken titles – which gives you an idea of just how far Wasps have come in recent years.

Their Heineken Cup final triumph over Toulouse was the culmination of a punishing work schedule put in place by Gatland, fellow coach Shaun Edwards and a fitness team headed by Craig White that has pushed everyone to the very limit. It was the pre-season work plus the constant fitness checks that gave Wasps the belief that they could live with whatever Toulouse threw at them in a hugely enjoyable final. Just listen to how the fitness regime changed wing Tom Voyce, whose try-scoring and superb running was to give Wasps a game-breaking ability they needed in those frantic final weeks of the season.

After arriving from Bath, Voyce discovered he was neither strong enough nor quick enough to satisfy the Wasps fitness crew. Voyce's weight rose from 87kg (13st 10lbs) to 93kg (14st 9lbs), and he won't rest until he reaches 100kg (15st 10lbs). 'Wasps took hold of me and said, "This is what you're going to do". The crucial start was in changing my physique. I'm feeling stronger and more confident. I wasn't as sharp as I should have been. Footwork drills have had me concentrating on my first three strides, which is something I'd never thought of. My speed off the mark has increased and it's given me a couple of seconds extra, which is very important.

'It worked and now I feel at the top of my game and there is more to come. It still hasn't sunk in that I have won so much with Wasps.'

This self-belief was tested to the full much earlier in the Heineken Cup when Wasps wobbled – to the consternation of their adoring fans. Wasps lost a pool match to the Celtic Warriors, and the 14-9 reverse suggested Dallaglio's men were going to come up short in a tournament they had never managed to dominate in previous attempts. Their only way back into contention in the pool was to go down to Bridgend less than a week later and pull off a revenge mission. That is exactly what Wasps achieved, defeating the now defunct Welsh outfit 17-12 in a match that showed just how cussed they could be when the situation required that kind of attitude.

The Celtic defeat was one of just four the club suffered in a 26-match run from their loss to Leicester on 8 November, and that is title-winning consistency. The first week of February proved

ABOVE Tense moments for Wasps in the semi-finals as Jim Williams scores for Munster.

RIGHT Man of the match Joe Worsley halts Finau Maka in the final at Twickenham.

PAGES 104-105 The Wasps squad celebrate.

to be absolutely crucial in the club's bid to end the season with another double to match their Parker Pen Challenge Cup and Zurich Play-off final successes of the previous campaign.

In seven days, Dallaglio took his men to Perpignan in the last Heineken Cup pool match and to Bath – the Zurich Premiership leaders – and came away with two absolutely critical wins. It was the kind of psychological lift you cannot quantify and, at the same time, it sent a clear message to the rest of Europe that the reigning English champions were the real deal in the biggest tournament in the northern hemisphere.

Former Wasps director of rugby Nigel Melville had to bring his Gloucester team to Wycombe for the Heineken Cup quarter-final, but somewhere along the way they got lost. Wasps cruised to a 34-3 victory – something that should never have been possible against the kind of forward threat the West Country side normally posed. But who cares? Wasps were happy to take a simple win given the looming end-of-season log jam of massively difficult fixtures.

The Heineken Cup semi-finals put Wasps up against Munster while the all-French affair across the Channel was to involve holders Toulouse – still to hit their stride – and big-spending Biarritz. Toulouse were too good on the day and claimed their place in the final at Twickenham. All they had to do was wait to see who emerged victorious in Dublin.

The scene that Munster's army of red-clad fans created at the old Lansdowne Road stadium will not be forgotten by those lucky enough to get into the ground. Around 2,000 Wasps fans made the trip and they were completely shouted down by the Munster men and women, who believed this was going to be their year. However, they had not counted on facing a team that was operating at the very peak of its powers, and an early Josh Lewsey try proved that the London side had a cutting edge Munster could not blunt. When they lost outside half Ronan O'Gara, the game was up, and with ex-Wales scrum half Rob Howley charging down a kick for veteran flanker Paul Volley to touch down, the champions of England were on their way to a 'home' final courtesy of a 37-32 win in what many have declared to be the finest Heineken Cup match ever staged.

The massive high created by the Dublin heroics was undermined by successive Zurich defeats by Gloucester and Leicester, and it was with much trepidation that Wasps fans headed to Twickenham. After all, Toulouse were the Manchester United of European rugby while Wasps operated on a much smaller wage bill and squad. Could they regain that winning feeling and prove that 15 like-minded souls who were fitter than the opposition could make rugby history?

Thanks to Joe Worsley's man-of-the-match performance and a brilliant late solo try from Rob Howley allied to Mark Van Gisbergen's 17 points, the Wasps fans were able to celebrate an outstanding 27-20 victory at a packed Twickenham. Club owner Chris Wright, who fell in love with Wasps after initially taking them into his Loftus Road family as a business venture, was on the pitch to see his men parade the trophy that signalled their arrival as the Kings of Europe.

At the heart of their success was that man Dallaglio, who immediately set new goals for the club that has been such a huge part of his adult life. He said: 'To repeat what Leicester managed – back-to-back cups – would be something very special. We have won successive Zurich Premiership titles and we are not trying to run before we can walk in terms of the Heineken competition. We are going to enjoy this first cup success and then look at ways of trying to repeat it next season.

'One thing is for sure, it's not going to get any easier to win the cup.'

With full back Van Gisbergen, formerly of Waikato, showing the kind of class England may be able to call on next year when he qualifies and Worsley earning the man-of-the-match award for his thunderous tackling, Wasps did just enough to beat the Heineken Cup holders.

Fabien Pelous accused Wasps of 'cheating cleverly', but Dallaglio dismissed this as sour grapes and also shrugged his shoulders when it was suggested the ball had nudged the touch line as it rolled forward for Howley to score the winning try. At the end of a cup campaign that required Wasps to win away at Perpignan, Celtic Warriors and Munster, the England captain insisted his men deserved a bit of luck. In truth, this wasn't about luck. Wasps were Heineken Cup champions and merited every plaudit that came their way.

The final word goes to that man Worsley, who cut Toulouse down with his brilliant tackles. He said: 'After the Munster game we had a couple of disappointing performances and that was a come down, but this was a final and a totally different situation.

'Our line out and first phase possession was pretty appalling against Toulouse, yet we still won and just imagine what this team would be capable of if we got it all right. The next 12 months will be very interesting.'

SARACENS FOUNDATION

REGISTERED CHARITY No. 1079316

Sport for Health

ENHANCING THE LIVES OF CHILDREN & YOUNG PEOPLE THROUGH SPORT

To find out more about the work of the **Saracens Foundation** and how you can support visit **www.saracens.com** or call us on **01923 204 601**

Quins' New Love Affair
the 2004 Parker Pen Cup Final

by TERRY COOPER

'Ten years ago Dick Best, then coaching Harlequins, said that the club had "a love affair with the cup". He meant the English domestic cup.... Now they have a new love – this Parker Pen event ...'

Good old Jason Leonard! You can always rely on him. His beloved Harlequins are trailing by six points in the Parker Pen Challenge Cup final against Montferrand at the Madejski Stadium. It's inside the final minute. They are defending frantically near their own line. Now, you couldn't expect Jason to run the length of the field for the winning try, in the same way that you did not expect him to do a Jonny Wilkinson and drop the goal that won the World Cup. But what he did was just as match-winning. He got himself whacked – and the rest of the team, dripping with relief, exploited the resultant penalty to achieve the crucial seven points for victory. What a noble act by Jason in the final seconds of his dedicated 14 years with the multi-coloured club. Whatever he did, it incited the mad Frenchman to attack him, and if the bruises on his face were all the colours of the shirt, he wore them with pride. His legacy to his colleagues is major rugby in Europe.

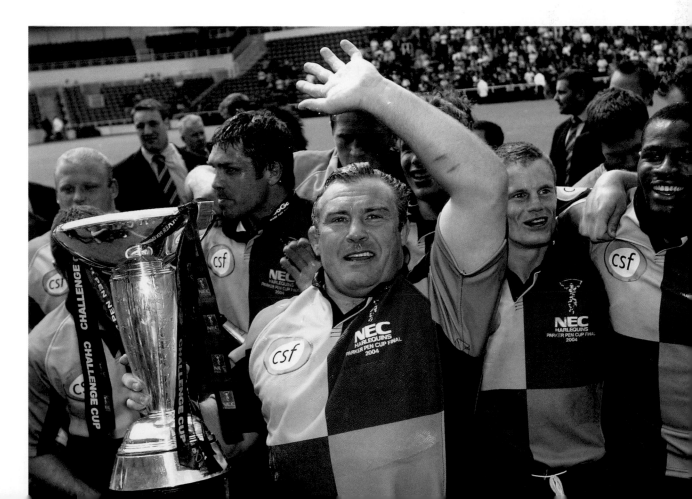

PAGE 107 And it's goodbye from him ... Jason Leonard with the Parker Pen Challenge Cup after his final game for Quins.

BELOW Mel Deane tackles Montferrand centre Raphael Chanal, who was later red-carded following his attack on Jason Leonard.

RIGHT Simon Keogh scampers home for the winning try.

Ten years ago Dick Best, then coaching Harlequins, said that the club had 'a love affair with the cup'. He meant the English domestic cup. He was comparing their displays in knockout with their league efforts. They won the cup in 1988 and 1991 and were runners-up on three other occasions. Their best placing in the league is third. Now they have a new love – this Parker Pen event for teams who fail to qualify for the Heineken Cup. They have triumphed twice now, having also taken the trophy in 2001. The tournament is erroneously regarded as markedly inferior to the Heineken. But each year there are many quality teams competing in it and at least in the later stages the rugby is as skilled and intense as the nominally senior tournament. And, of course, there is much, much more than the cup for the winners, who are elevated into the admittedly more lucrative Heineken.

Since the final whistle at Madejski there has been a feel-good factor at Harlequins. Mark Evans, who wears a tracksuit as coach and a City suit as chief executive, tries to play the blasé card by saying, 'We were interested in the final for itself and not as a means to any other end. There is a powerful motivation not to lose any rugby match – let alone a final. Supporters and players like to win things. One last play turned a good season into a memorable one. Few here will forget that afternoon at Madejski. On the day and throughout the season it was a terrific achievement. Look who won it in 2003 – only Wasps, who have proved the best team in Europe this time round. Financially, it does not make a huge amount of difference, but, even with the development of our Stoop Ground, we cannot increase capacity much yet. It's going up by just 1,000 in the autumn. We will sell the extra season tickets. But from the club-building aspect it's very helpful. From the rugby viewpoint it's where everybody wants to be. We have the chance to host and visit the great clubs of this competition – Toulouse, Cardiff, Llanelli, Munster and our annual rivals Wasps, Leicester and Gloucester. We are certainly in much better shape to be competitive this time than on our last time in the big boys' tournament. And it certainly makes it easier to recruit from outside England when we can offer them the Heineken

challenge. When we were trailing round Europe looking after our results, we all looked at what was going on in the Heineken very wistfully. It would be nice to be there, we thought – and now we are.'

The finish to that Reading final was entirely appropriate, as the previous 79 minutes of the match had been full of drama and fluctuations, with Harlequins' winning score being the fifth time they had led. After early penalties, Will Greenwood's cross-field chip was safely collected by Gavin Duffy for the opening try. Olivier Azam put Montferrand ahead thanks to the TV ref, then an exchange of kicks spanning half-time left Quins 17-16 in front. But the French team had already revealed their indiscipline when flanker Marc Raynaud was binned by referee Nigel Whitehouse for entering a ruck illegally. By the hour Montferrand led 23-17 after scrum half Pierre Mignoni was mauled over.

They deserved that lead, but they did not deserve the cup, because one reckless, violent player single-handedly, or single-fistedly, squandered the prize. Enter centre Raphael Chanal. He was yellow-carded for a punch, and substitute Andy Dunne banked the points from the resultant penalty. Re-enter Chanal after ten minutes that patently did little to calm him down. His 14 colleagues had 'drawn' the period when he was in the bin, so that they led 26-20 – and he betrayed them. As Quins desperately tried to gain possession at a ruck, Chanal ran to the breakdown and punched Leonard twice. Red card for a second offence. Quins ran the ball, recycling it through many hands and found the gap just where Chanal should have been defending. Wings George Harder and Ugo Monye linked to give sub Simon Keogh space for a joyous run behind the posts. The conversion was theoretically simple, but so much rested on the extra points. Deep breath for Dunne and he did the job – 27-26 to Quins.

Gentleman Jason's first words were of sorrow for his assailant. 'It is not pleasurable to have an opponent sent off, even when it leads to such an important score.' Coach Evans reflected: 'We were never more than a score adrift, but inside that last minute I thought the cup was probably gone. I should have had more faith, because we had succeeded in tight finishes recently. We have a positive attitude arising from a sort of rebirth of the club four years ago. The players are all committed to each other. It is a tightknit squad, who prove that will and spirit can overcome most things – as you witnessed.'

Powergen is proud to support all
levels of English club rugby

powergen.co.uk

REVIEW OF THE
SEASON 2003-04

England Eclipsed the 2004 Six Nations Championship

by CHRIS JONES

'After two away wins, England returned to Twickenham for their first home international as world champions and promptly crashed to a shock 19-13 defeat to Ireland ...'

England head coach Clive Woodward was able, with hindsight, to identify the problems that undermined the World Cup winners' failed defence of their RBS Six Nations Grand Slam. England finished third after losing to France and Ireland, and Woodward lamented, 'What happened in the Six Nations did not surprise me. We got what we deserved. The major factor was our lack of training days. We weren't prepared anywhere near as well as we normally are.'

What Woodward later accepted – after a disastrous tour of New Zealand and Australia – was his failure to properly plan for the retirement of captain Martin Johnson after the World Cup triumph and of Neil Back and Jason Leonard during the championship. Of course, there was also the small matter of a missing superstar at No. 10.

With the injured Jonny Wilkinson joining Johnson on the unavailable list and key players showing wear and tear – mentally and physically – after the cup campaign, then the Six Nations was an accident waiting to happen for England.

While those points are put forward to explain England's problems, they do not detract from the excellence of a fourth slam for France in the past eight years. There was a wobble at the end for Bernard Laporte's men when they let a big lead collapse against England at the Stade de France, but the best team in the championship claimed all the honours.

Scrum half Dimitri Yachvili, who finished with a personal tally of 19 points

LEFT Josh Lewsey is unceremoniously dumped by Frédéric Michalak at Stade de France.

RIGHT Will Greenwood just fails to touch down for England v Ireland at Twickenham.

in the 24-21 win, was the dominating factor in the match which saw Imanol Harinordoquy show considerable nerve in waiting for the bounce and calmly claiming it for the early try. Yachvili, of Biarritz, whose Georgian-born father Michel hooked for France in the late 1960s, claimed a try of his own when he kicked the loose ball down the blind side and won the chase by yards to touch down.

England may have held the World Cup, but the French were once again the champions of Europe. To some extent this helped erase from the memory the desperate French performance in the World Cup semi-final against the English in a rain-soaked Sydney the previous November.

The French campaign had started in confident fashion with a 35-17 home win over fancied Ireland in Paris. The Irish were supposed to be the coming team in the championship, thanks to their big pack and the brilliance of Brian O'Driscoll at centre, but it was to prove to be a mixed Six Nations for Eddie O'Sullivan's men. They would eventually pick up the Triple Crown, having beaten England at Twickenham, but the ultimate European title was to elude them once again.

While Ireland were losing at Stade de France, Woodward's rearranged England side were scoring 50 points to Italy's 9 at the Stadio Flaminio to suggest that they could achieve something important despite the key men who were missing.

Jason Robinson, asked to fill the outside-centre position lying vacant because of Mike Tindall's ankle injury, responded with a hat-trick of tries. Paul Grayson scored 20 points as Wilkinson's understudy, while Chris Jones, the lanky Sale flanker, made a try-scoring debut as a replacement.

England headed to Scotland a week later and registered a 35-13 win in a match remembered more for Woodward's anger over the pre-match programme the Scots inflicted upon their visitors. Flames flickered from the stands, three pipers played from the roofs, while more pipers carpeted the pitch, forcing England to sidestep their way through the massed ranks to make open ground. The match itself produced a host of 'own tries', with mistakes by both teams proving costly before England captain Lawrence Dallaglio collected the Calcutta Cup.

After two away wins, England returned to Twickenham for their first home international as world champions and promptly crashed to a shock 19-13 defeat to Ireland which ended Woodward's 22-game unbeaten run at HQ. The week had started with the announcement by Jason Leonard that he would be quitting international rugby at the end of the Six Nations after taking his world record number of caps to 114 over 14 seasons of international duty. With Neil Back following suit, England were losing more experience than they ever thought possible just months after tasting World Cup success. Allied to the shock of losing to Ireland, it left the England squad looking more vulnerable than at any time since the 1999 World Cup quarter-final defeat by South Africa.

Ireland triumphed through the boot of Ronan O'Gara and Girvan Dempsey's try, but it was Gordon D'Arcy, playing outstandingly well in the centre, who not only eclipsed O'Driscoll but proved he was a star in his own right. Paul O'Connell's excellent line-out work made England hooker Steve Thompson look second rate. The latter's throwing-in went to pot and it was to be a problem all season.

On the same day in Rome, Italy were proving they could still produce a shock – even if it was against a poor Scotland – registering a 20-14 win. It was a result that would consign the Scots to the Wooden Spoon; the improved form they were eventually to show on tour in Australia was a long way off. The hard-hitting Andrea De Rossi and the outstanding Sergio Parisse at No. 8, were the stars for the home side, with Roland De Marigny kicking five penalties.

With news of England's setback boosting their own cause, the French arrived in Cardiff and fashioned a 29-22 victory through man of the match Jean-Baptiste Elissalde, who scored 24 points from scrum half. Wales relied on the boot of out-half Stephen Jones, playing to rigid percentages, with their open-field running saved for the final five minutes when replacement back-row Martyn Williams finally breached the visitors' line for a try.

Wales took enough from this game to believe they could follow Ireland's lead and make it successive home defeats for England. However, an early line-out mistake allowed Ben Cohen to score his 27th try in 39 Tests, and Olly Barkley, at No. 10, kicked the conversion to allow the home fans to believe normal service would be restored. The 31-21 final score showed that England were still vulnerable, but at least they had a win to take with them for the slam showdown in Paris.

Wales, who had earlier beaten Scotland 23-10, finished the season with a 44-10 win over Italy to prove that they could still produce try-scoring talent behind a pack that was also showing signs of being competitive when at full strength. The victory also allowed Steve Hansen to make a winning farewell as the Wales coach before heading back to work with the All Blacks.

However, the Wales v Italy clash in Cardiff was merely a sideshow on the final day of the championship. Over in Dublin, Ireland had a big opportunity – and they made the most of it. True, they were facing a Scotland team that had continued its dreadful season with a 31-0 home loss to the French, but this fixture is always feisty. The Irish took due note of this and imposed themselves with authority to give their fans a seventh Triple Crown in 107 years of trying, and a first since 1985.

Again, it was that man D'Arcy who grabbed the headlines and set out his stall for a place on the Lions tour to New Zealand in 2005. D'Arcy scored two of Ireland's five tries in a 37-16 win. Scotland lost outstanding No. 8 Simon Taylor with a serious knee ligament injury just minutes into the second half and conceded 21 points in the last half hour to make it a season to forget.

Ireland enjoyed a lap of honour on the Lansdowne turf and then joined the rest of the Six Nations in turning their attention to Paris, where a late-night kick-off made it impossible for fans who had travelled from England to get home that night. That pushed up the cost of the trip and continued to fuel the debate over how much influence television should have over fixture scheduling. When the French fans had finished cheering their slam winners they joined the thousands racing to the local stations to try and catch the last train into the city.

The Six Nations continues to be a superb tournament, but outside influences are changing the face of the jewel in the northern hemisphere rugby crown. Sunday rugby, staggered kick-offs and even the suggestion of Friday rugby is going to hurt the Six Nations – and you tamper with the tournament at your peril.

PAGE **115** Jean-Baptiste Elissalde sprints for the line to score v Wales at Cardiff.

BELOW Fabio Ongaro registers the only try of the match as Italy beat Scotland in Rome.

The Club Scene
England: An Outstanding Year

by **BILL MITCHELL**

'Yet England's World Cup triumph should not be allowed to eclipse the successes seen on the club stage, most notably the European victories of Wasps … and Harlequins …'

England enjoyed an outstanding season with victory in the World Cup the climax – and the ultimate success was well merited. In fact it overshadowed everything else. Yet the drop from the heady heights to third place in the subsequent Six Nations tournament should have surprised no one, as there had been some critical absences through retirement and injury, notably the inspirational skipper Martin Johnson (stepped down from the international scene) and the kicking hero Jonny Wilkinson (crocked). England's dependence on Wilkinson can be illustrated by the fact that of the 72 points scored by his side in the knockout stages of the World Cup tournament, he recorded a massive 62, England in the same matches having scored two tries to their opponents' five!

If one adds to the success of the fifteens team the fact that England's sevens squad ended the IRB Series as very honourable runners-up to New Zealand, then it could be said that most things in the house were extremely satisfactory (club scene included), with one notable exception that proved that no one can be perfect.

BELOW Just one more time … Jonny Wilkinson's boot sends the winning dropped goal on its way, 22 November 2003.

100,000 product lines
730 branches
One merchant kicks the others into touch

Travis Perkins is one of the UK's leading suppliers of timber, building materials, plumbing & heating and tool hire.

For details of your nearest branch call 0800 389 6611.

Travis Perkins

www.travisperkins.co.uk

Pleased to support The Wooden Spoon Society Rugby World 2004

The Six Nations campaign was followed by a summer tour that was a sad anticlimax, particularly as the area chosen was Australasia, where the local heroes had points to prove. To face the inevitable tough challenge, the strongest possible side just was not available, and the results were a national disaster, with defeats against New Zealand (36-3 and 36-12) and Australia (51-15). In only one of the threesome was there a valid excuse – in the second encounter with the All Blacks the team had to play a man short for an hour thanks to the harsh dismissal of lock Simon Shaw, who was later exonerated by a disciplinary hearing. The same panel, however, gave another lock, Danny Grewcock, a ten-match ban for foul play perpetrated soon after he entered the fray as a replacement. All of this obscured the fact that England had played bravely against the odds and deserved better from the match, which could not be said about the other defeats. However, all teams have to rebuild at some stage.

Yet England's World Cup triumph should not be allowed to eclipse the successes seen on the club stage, most notably the European victories of Wasps in the Heineken Cup and Harlequins in the Parker Pen Cup. Both came after thrilling finals and were aided, it must be said, by some good fortune – but that is the name of the game. Poor French discipline was a major contributory factor in both matches.

Wasps were probably again the best club side in Europe, but their domestic success must be measured against the fact that Bath, the side they beat in the Zurich Championship final, finished top of the league table. So for the second season, Wasps were proclaimed champions after another side had done better in the hard graft of a league season. It was analagous to unbeaten Arsenal being asked to take part in one-off play-offs for the soccer Premiership then losing the title to a side that had finished below them in the table. It is surely not beyond the ingenuity of officialdom to arrive at a logical solution to this anomaly. Two trophies, perhaps? Why not? At the other end of the table, meanwhile, poor Rotherham were outclassed and provided a good excuse for those who opposed their promotion to the top flight in the first place.

In the National League, top spot in division one went to the consistent Worcester outfit, who won all of their 26 matches; Orrell came an excellent second, while the bottom clubs, Manchester and Wakefield (on points difference), did not disgrace themselves. In division two Sedgley Park just edged out Nottingham in a cliffhanger, with Lydney at the foot of the table being slightly out of their depth. The two third divisions provided further excitement, with the North title going to Halifax by two points from Waterloo, and another famous name – Blackheath – just shading the South section on points difference from the gallant men from Cornwall – Launceston.

Wasps were unable to extend their successes to include the Powergen Cup, as they made the mistake of underestimating their quarter-final visitors, Pertemps Bees from Birmingham. They were narrowly ousted from a competition that eventually was won by Newcastle at Twickenham after an absolutely outstanding final against Sale, who were overtaken in the match's closing stages to go down narrowly 37-33. This was but one final on a day when the spectators had a surfeit of entertainment, with Bristol winning the Powergen Challenge Shield against Waterloo (53-24), Bradford and Bingley the same sponsors' Intermediate Cup against Gloucester Old Boys (46-18) and Leodiensian their Junior Vase as a result of a two-to-one try count after a drawn match with North Ribblesdale (13-13). It was a pity that this day was not the climax of the season, but such occasions are a great festival outing for everyone, as the Scots originally discovered.

Elsewhere the Barbarians continued to fly their excellent entertaining flag with their usual very helpful – for the opposition – programme, which included matches against Scotland, Wales (an embarrassing defeat) and England. Oxford will rue the fact that they could again have won the Varsity Match had some players not tried to be heroes when passes to better-placed colleagues might have brought dividends against a brave Cambridge defence. It ended in an 11-11 draw – the first dead heat since 1965 – and in terms of matches against the old enemy in 2004 it was the only one not won by the Dark Blues.

Durham won an excellent BUSA final against the gallant resistance of Exeter University, while The Army beat the Royal Navy in the deciding Inter-Services match at Twickenham (the Royal Air Force now finds it difficult to find good enough players to make an adequate challenge). The women's game flourishes, with France just a better international outfit than England in European terms and Wasps (league champions), Clifton (runners-up) and Saracens (cup winners) the best club sides at the moment.

Altogether it provides a very healthy outlook, and if other nations in Europe can mount a credible challenge to the apparent present superiority of England and France no one can really complain.

RIGHT Ian McInroy (No. 13) congratulates Charlie Desmond on his score in the 72nd minute of the Varsity Match. The Cambridge wing's try brought the scoreline to 11-11 and enabled Cambridge, as holders, to retain the MMC Trophy.

LEFT The Leodiensian team celebrate victory in the final of the Junior Vase on Powergen finals day at HQ in April.

PAGE 119 Bristol's James Bailey gives the Waterloo Drummers defence the slip as the Shoguns tirumph in the Powergen Challenge Shield final.

BELOW Ireland captain Brian O'Driscoll looks for a gap in the England defence during the Barbarians' 32-12 victory at Twickenham at the end of May.

Scotland: Hawks Sweep the Board

by ALAN LORIMER

'Undoubtedly much of Hawks' success is down to the coaching team of former British Lions Peter Wright and Bob Ackerman. Wright as head coach made sure that for once Hawks were entirely focused on the job in hand.'

If it was a miserable season for Scotland on the international stage, then the performances in the Celtic League of the three Scottish professional teams – Edinburgh, Glasgow and The Borders – provided little comfort. In that order they finished tenth, eleventh and twelfth. Or to put it more bluntly, third last, second last, and, yes, last.

Defenders of the professional teams have always claimed that success was secondary to the primary role of providing players for the national team, and therefore results were not paramount. Moreover, the professional clubs themselves would claim that, financially, they were not on a par with their Celtic League rivals. Money to an extent, goes the argument, can buy success. Lack of it produces the kind of league finishes that have characterised the Scottish professional clubs.

That, however, is all about to change. The cash-strapped, debt-ridden Scottish Rugby Union in their recently announced four-year strategy have advocated removing the dead hand of central control and want the Scottish pro teams to be franchised out, to be self-supporting and to be successful. What is more, contracted players will no longer be on a gravy train. The new dictum is all about win bonuses, about players genuinely earning their wages. Tough talk, but the feeling is that it is an overdue message.

Given that the age of enlightened thinking has not descended on Scottish rugby until now, it was still creditable that twelfth-placed Borders produced Scotland scrum half Chris Cusiter, Edinburgh brought Ally Hogg, Tom Philip, Simon Webster, and Hugo Southwell to the fore, and Glasgow revealed the talents of Graeme Morrison, Donnie Macfadyen, Sean Lamont and Dan Parks.

All of these players grabbed their chances during the period of the World Cup, when life in the Celtic League continued as normally as it could with so many top players absent. Of the three professional sides in Scotland, it was Edinburgh who were most affected by World Cup call-ups, but their reserve brigade still produced five victories during RWC.

Edinburgh's best run was outwith the Celtic League. In the Celtic Cup they reached the final, only to lose to Ulster at Murrayfield; and in the Heineken Cup Edinburgh became the first Scottish club to reach the quarter-finals.

The capital's Heineken victories included a useful win over the eventual runners-up, Toulouse, in the pool stages. But in the quarters the Edinburgh side again met Toulouse, and this time were heavily defeated by the pedigree French club.

Much of the Edinburgh success has been rightly attributed to the leadership, the coaching skills and the sheer playing ability of the former New Zealand captain Todd Blackadder. So impressive was the quietly spoken Blackadder, that he was appointed assistant to new Scotland coach Matt Williams. Blackadder, however, dispelled any notion that he was hanging up his boots by quickly announcing his intention to resume playing for Edinburgh next season.

Edinburgh's worst run was during the Six Nations, when their squad became so depleted by Scotland call-ups that amateur players were called in as cover. In the event the gap between amateur and professional rugby was cruelly exposed, and Edinburgh suffered. The upside, however, was that a number of amateur players were given a taste of the professional game, and in the process gained a foothold on the ladder.

For Glasgow, there was a new coaching set-up, with former Scotland centre Sean Lineen and international lock Shade Munro brought in as assistants to Hugh Campbell. But despite an injection of new talent on both the coaching and playing sides, Glasgow manifestly failed to impress, despite an encouraging opening win over Cardiff at Hughenden. Nor was there much to cheer about in the knockout competitions. Glasgow were unable to make a mark in the Parker Pen Challenge Cup or the Shield, and in the Celtic Cup they had an undistinguished run.

Individually, former Dollar Academy and Glasgow Hawks centre Graeme Morrison, a powerhouse of a player, quickly established

LEFT Hawks centre Colin Shaw crosses for a try despite the efforts of Nick De Luca, as the Glasgow side beat Heriot's to clinch the Premier League title.

BELOW Edinburgh's Simon Webster slips past Patrice Collazo of Toulouse in the Heineken Cup quarter-finals. The capital side were the first Scottish team to reach this point in the competition but went down despite a win against the Frenchmen in the pool stage.

himself as a first-team regular in his first season as a professional, before becoming part of the Scotland squad and earning a first cap during the Scots tour of Australia.

Glasgow's player of the year, however, was the winger Sean Lamont. Signed by Glasgow from Rotherham and having impressed hugely in the Scotland sevens side, Lamont transferred the skills learnt in the abbreviated code to the fifteens game with considerable success, before joining Morrison on the Scotland tour Down Under.

It was perhaps inevitable that The Borders finished last in the Celtic League and last in the domestic tussle for Heineken Cup places. Underfunded to a greater degree than the city siblings, The Borders never had the front-line talent or the depth to compete seriously.

Not even the coaching experience of former All Blacks assistant Tony Gilbert could work the necessary magic on a squad which he admitted was seriously short of class players. Matters were made worse by the exit of Gregor Townsend, who, on being informed that he was not in national coach Matt Williams's plans for the Scotland squad, decided to accept a short-term Super 12 contract with The Sharks in Durban.

The Borders' coach also inherited a number of players not wanted by the other two districts, who would not have been on his shopping list. Now Gilbert, after overseeing the first two years of The Borders' existence, has handed over to the former Wasps and England scrum half Steve Bates, who previously coached Newcastle.

Welsh-born Bates has insisted that his new side will attempt to take on both Edinburgh and Glasgow, even if The Borders are operating on a smaller budget. 'There is no question of playing second fiddle to Edinburgh and Glasgow. Our aim is to win the Celtic League and if that means beating Edinburgh and Glasgow then so be it,' he said.

Bates will have a number of players in his squad either on the fringe of or in the Scotland set-up. Chris Cusiter heads this list, which also includes lock Scott MacLeod, full back Gareth Morton, centre/wing Stephen Cranston and hooker Ross Ford.

Cusiter would be the first to admit that he learned volumes from that legend of Scottish rugby Gary Armstrong. The former Scotland and Lions scrum half at the age of 37 finally bowed out of professional rugby, his inspiring performance in The Borders' Heineken Cup win over Agen at Netherdale being a fitting memory to retain of this greatest of great players.

There has been in Scotland a concern that the gap between the professional sides and the top end of the amateur game is too great. The strategic review has recommended that an elite layer of eight teams should be created that would allow the top amateurs to be concentrated in a small league. This, says the review, would test these players in a near professional environment while at the same time increasing the pool of players from which the national side could be selected.

To an extent, a number of the top amateur teams have anticipated such a move by becoming near semi-professional sides, certainly in attitude if not exactly in monetary terms. None exemplified more this attitudinal approach than Glasgow Hawks, who achieved a BT League/Cup double in an almost faultless season.

Undoubtedly much of Hawks' success is down to the coaching team of former British Lions Peter Wright and Bob Ackerman. Wright as head coach made sure that for once Hawks were entirely focused on the job in hand. In their bad old days it used to be said of the Anniesland club 'When the going gets tough, Hawks go skiing'.

Not any more. Wright, a former blacksmith before becoming an SRU development officer, forged a new attitude in a side that had hitherto consistently underperformed. Moreover, the Hawks' policy of using home players and refusing to go down the route of buying in foreigners also paid off.

The two non-Scots were back-rower Mark Sitch, an Australian who came over to Scotland seven years ago, and Mike Rainey, last year's Ireland Under 21 stand-off, who is a student in Glasgow.

Hawks' closest challengers in the BT Premiership were Boroughmuir and Aberdeen GSFP, but disappointingly Watsonians, who had a penchant for South African players, and Heriot's faded in the later part of the season.

At the other end of the Premiership, Pccblcs wcrc relegated after a two-year spell in the top flight, and were joined by Stirling County. Meanwhile, Gala and Biggar fought off Dundee HSFP for the two promotion places from division two, but the Dundee club at least had the satisfaction of contesting the BT Cup final, albeit losing to the all-conquering Hawks.

The challenge for club rugby in Scotland remains constant. At the professional level, there must be improvements in standards to match the top Welsh and Irish sides; that, too, is the goal at the top end of the amateur game. But below this layer, one senses that in a country where competitive sport, after shamefully being allowed to decline in state schools, is an endangered species, rugby's priority is to establish once more a critical mass. This could be a crucial season for the game in Scotland.

Wales: Then There Were Four

by DAVID STEWART

'As the Celtic Warriors put their boots away – at least those not required for national duty in Argentina and South Africa – it was announced that the union had bought out this team. And promptly closed it down.'

It was meant to be a time of new beginnings; year zero for the professional end of the sport in Wales – a regional system in place, a reduction to five professional teams with consequent concentration of the available talent and finance. Llanelli Scarlets pipped Ulster to the first full home-and-away Celtic League, other Welsh teams filled the next four places and a structure at last seemed in place from which the game could move forward. Admittedly marketing of the new teams was underwhelming, efforts to develop a product in North Wales had a hint of tokenism, and there was a failure to imitate Ireland by centrally contracting key players – all represented opportunities missed by the WRU, but as the season ended it seemed the governing body had put the sport broadly back on the rails.

Then the bombshell dropped. As the Celtic Warriors put their boots away – at least those not required for national duty in Argentina and South Africa – it was announced that the union had bought out this team. And promptly closed it down. Result: a squad of players plus coaching and backroom staff desperate for new contracts elsewhere, but perhaps more seriously a real anger, tinged with cynicism, among the now long-suffering rugby public. True, the union had said a year earlier that five was a region too many (and some of the sharper commentators agreed), but now the good folk of the Bridgend/Mid-Glamorgan and Pontypridd/Rhondda areas had rather warmed to their combined side, even if crowds could have been higher at home games. A large element of the fan base flooded media outlets in protest at being disenfranchised, as they saw it, noting that their area has produced many of Wales's finest in recent years – the likes of Gibbs, Jenkins, Howley, Llewellyn and Thomas.

The bad odour this decision brought upon the game's rulers merely compounded their folly surrounding the appointment of Mike Ruddock. Not that supporters consider the former Newport Gwent Dragons boss as anything other than a worthy successor to Steve Hansen, but he had publicly ruled himself out, and a shortlist of Gareth Jenkins and Mark Evans emerged amid newspaper leaks from HQ as to their respective prospects. On the day set for formally announcing the new man, Ruddock was produced at a press conference – only for Jenkins, the expected choice, to proclaim his subsequent unhappiness at not being informed in advance. He went on to say he could not see himself as a candidate for the position again while the union is 'under its current management'. Once more the WRU had, in management and public-relations terms, scored rugby's equivalent of an own goal.

Sadly it seemed so unnecessary and served only to cloud progress on other fronts. The national team recovered from a Six Nations 'whitewash' in 2003 to put up an encouraging World Cup showing and produce two home wins in this year's championship. What we previously called the club scene is now more accurately referred to as the regional one. A cause for concern is that despite their strong showing in the Celtic League, Welsh teams continued to disappoint in the more demanding environment of the Heineken Cup.

Again, the Scarlets were the sole standard-bearers in qualifying from the group stages; indeed no others even came close. Having lost at home a year earlier to Perpignan in the knockout stages, Llanelli this time came unstuck against Biarritz and their jumbo rolling-maul-specialist pack. Ever the realist, coach Gareth Jenkins admitted afterwards that 'looking at those left in the competition, at this stage of our development we are a quarter-final team'. Qualification was achieved courtesy of a crucial away win at Northampton (headlined by young full back Barry Davies's stunning individual try), but a repetition will be needed next term as the two teams have once again been drawn together.

LEFT Brent Cockbain collects for Celtic Warriors v Wasps at the Causeway Stadium, High Wycombe. The Warriors won this Heineken Cup clash 14-9 and finished fourth in the Celtic League, but at the end of the season the club was closed and their 2004-05 Heineken Cup place passed to Cardiff Blues.

The Scarlets' league triumph was achieved in the most exciting of circumstances. Matches were predominantly played on a Friday night, and in sunny mid-May more than 12,000 crowded into Stradey Park to watch the likely showdown with rivals Ulster, who were chasing a double, having already captured the Celtic Cup. Such was the closeness of the arithmetic that Newport Gwent Dragons (the name of the town having been controversially added to their title in mid-season), playing in Dublin against Leinster, had a chance to take the honours. A 23-16 win by Llanelli, however, saw the trophy come to Wales for the first time, Leinster and Munster being the previous winners. It represented

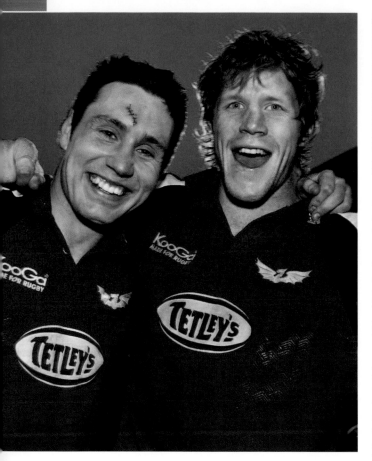

LEFT Stephen Jones and Simon Easterby celebrate the Llanelli Scarlets' 23-16 home win over Ulster that brought the Celtic League title to Stradey Park. Departing fly half Jones scored 18 points and created a try for Matthew Watkins.

BELOW RIGHT Dragons favourite Percy Montgomery reels in Leon Lloyd of the Tigers during Leicester's 26-20 Heineken victory at Rodney Parade. The South African's international career was revived in the summer, including a home cap against Wales.

a terrific effort over a 22-match programme by a squad that had lost so many players to the World Cup and Six Nations campaigns. Veteran Scott Quinnell recognised as much: 'The biggest thing coaches have learned is the need to manage squads throughout the season, you need 30 to 35 players if you are to win the league.' Jenkins in turn paid tribute to his other experienced players no longer in the international game, namely Chris Wyatt, John Davies, and skipper Vernon Cooper.

A worry for supporters is that an ageing bunch, particularly at forward, do not have an obvious succession line. True, the departure of the outstanding Stephen Jones (to the curious destination of Montferrand) will be overcome from within by Gareth Bowen, but in the fallout of players following the Warriors' dissolution the Scarlets were not aggressive recruiters.

Others were, and some, like Cardiff Blues, had to be. A back line of real pace and skill was regularly undermined by an ineffective platform. Hopefully the addition of such as Gethin Jenkins and Robert Sidoli will help their at times beleaguered coach, Dai Young, turn this around. The Robinson brothers had a good 12 months, but the prospect of forming a dashing midfield trio with Iestyn Harris next time around was dashed when the former rugby league maestro unhappily – some would say rather weakly – decided to return to his roots. His abundant handling and kicking skills never quite camouflaged a suspect front-on defence, but his departure takes an element of excitement with it. The Blues did not make the same fist of being a stand-alone team (not having previously merged with another club) as the Scarlets. The pressure will be on their management to deliver in 2004-05, especially since having originally been consigned to the Parker Pen Cup, the Warriors' demise gave Cardiff an eleventh-hour entry to the Heineken. Ironic that, since their respective chairmen only a few months earlier were discussing a merger between the two neighbouring regions – ultimately called off in the face of supporter opposition.

The Dragons were expected to struggle, with their players coming mainly from Newport and an uninspiring Ebbw Vale, but the excellent Ruddock – himself a native of north Gwent – chiselled out a tough, competitive pack with an effective if limited game plan. His priceless remark after the September win over Neath-Swansea Ospreys summed up their attitude: 'Not bad for a bunch of misfits'. Inspired by Percy Montgomery behind and Jason Forster up front, they fashioned a formidable home record, which included the European scalps of Stade Français and Ulster. The South African won the admiration of all by staying at Rodney Parade and training during his ban (imposed for an incident involving a touch judge at the end of the previous season and lasting until November) when the management had offered him a chance to return to his sunnier homeland. A note of aggravation was the Dragons' failure to take fixtures elsewhere, a foolish approach with arenas such as Pontypool Park and the Cwmbran Stadium available in the region, and one which alienated some of the potential fan base. An end-of-season hiccup saw Declan Kidney appointed to take over as coach, then his prompt (and surely questionable, having committed himself) switch to Leinster and the installation in the post of Chris Anderson, formerly coach of Australia's rugby league side. One new and useful talent available to him will be scrum half Gareth Cooper, a possible Lion in 2005. The Newport club, containing a hard core of their former professionals, won the new 16-club semi-pro Premiership division.

The Ospreys may be the team to watch. A merger of such historic rivals was always going to take time to bed down, but they can look forward to a new home in the Morfa Stadium conveniently located on the east fringes of Swansea, are getting their act together in the promotional sense, and have recruited well to a mainly young squad under the innovative Lyn Jones. A sluggish first half to last term saw radical surgery midway through, with captain Scott Gibbs retiring and old soldier Gareth Llewellyn being sidelined. But with talents like Shane Williams and Gavin Henson to be complemented by Sonny Parker and Brent Cockbain, the future could well be black and white. Former international hooker Barry Williams has been confirmed as captain, leaving an interesting dilemma regarding the promising giant Huw Bennett. A pleasing bonus to their year end was Neath beating Caerphilly in the final of the Principality Cup.

So now the WRU have their preferred option of four regions making up the professional game in Wales in the new season. The fervent wish of the paying and the television supporter is that at last the politics and off-the-field activities will take a back seat and the rugby itself predominate. Quinnell provides hope: 'A Celtic League side will win the Heineken in the next two or three years.' Maybe a Welsh one!

Ireland: Punching Above Their Weight
by SEAN DIFFLEY

'But, of course, the outstanding accomplishment was by Munster in yet again reaching the Heineken Cup semi-final stage, and then … producing against Wasps one of the very best matches ever in the competition.'

Overall, considering the resources available in a country in which rugby is very much the poor relation to Gaelic games and soccer, it was a good season for the Irish clubs and provinces in the Heineken Cup and the Celtic League and Cup. Apart from Ulster's triumph in the Celtic Cup, there was the now almost inevitable Munster appearance in the latter stages of the European event, and Connacht put in a brave effort against eventual competition winners Harlequins in the semi-final of the Parker Pen.

It is worthy of mention that all of Harlequins' points in their 27-26 triumph over Montferrand in the final were scored by their Irish pair, Simon Keogh and Andy Dunne, the former Ireland Under

21 half backs. And mention of the Under 21s brings us to the 2004 Under 21 World Cup in Scotland, in which the Irish side performed with great distinction. Irish age-group teams have been flourishing over the past while, from schools internationals to Under 21.

But, of course, the outstanding accomplishment was by Munster in yet again reaching the Heineken Cup semi-final stage, and then, before a packed Lansdowne Road, producing against Wasps one of the very best matches ever in the competition. Wasps' sheer power told in the end to bring about a 37-32 victory, although the loss of Ronan O'Gara and of David Wallace considerably reduced Munster's challenge.

What is it about Munster that engenders such consistently powerful performances? For the most part they rely on their native resources and in recent times have produced some world-class players. But it's not just the quality and basic skills that underpins the success. The remarkable and pleasant horde of supporters is closer to the team than is the case with other sides. It's that support which galvanises Munster.

All of that is in puzzling contrast to the recent movements of Leinster, the side based on the city of Dublin and which has the largest number of clubs and players in Ireland. Yet even with such outstanding players as Brian O'Driscoll, Gordon D'Arcy and Malcolm O'Kelly, success on the European stage continues to elude Leinster. But aren't those players called upon for Irish squad duty? Indeed Leinster have that problem, but so have Munster.

PAGE 131 Ulster skipper Andy Ward shows off the Celtic Cup after his side's 27-21 final win over Edinburgh at Murrayfield.

RIGHT Pierre Lazies celebrates his last-minute dropped goal to give Trinity College victory over UL Bohemians in the AIL division two final.

BELOW The Cork defence cannot stop Stephen Keogh powering over for Shannon in the AIL division one final.

Mike Ruddock of Wales and Matt Williams of Scotland were the recent Leinster coaches and didn't manage to salvage them from near mediocrity. This past season of 2003-04, Gary Ella arrived from Australia, but things, if anything, 'dis-improved'. At the end of the season the Leinster Branch announced that 'Gary Ella steps down from the position of team coach'. Instead, Declan Kidney, the Corkman who began Munster's successful progress and who didn't appear too happy as Eddie O'Sullivan's assistant coach to Ireland, steps in to coach Leinster.

Meanwhile, as the 'big shots' concentrate on the international competitions the ordinary club scene is in some difficulty. The IRFU and the senior clubs are concerned that the clubs are suffering severe financial problems and are less than happy with the format of the AIB All Ireland League.

The winning club in this season's All Ireland was once again the Limerick side Shannon, with a young coach, Geoff Moylan, who guided them to their second title in his three-year reign. They beat their old rivals Cork Constitution 22-16 in the final, with replacement back-row Stephen Keogh scoring their try, but the real difference was the place-kicking of wing Tom Cregan, who kicked five penalty goals. Cork Constitution scored a try through wing Conan Healy, which was converted by out-half Conrad O'Sullivan. Leinster's scrum half, Brian O'Meara, entered proceedings late for his club and kicked three penalty goals. But it was not enough. In three of the past four All Ireland series, Cork Con have finished top of the division in the league part of the competition but have lost in the play-off finals.

That division one final was not the only offering at Lansdowne Road that afternoon. The powers that be had decided that all three finals should be played and that ensured a good spate of entertainment. In the second division final, Dublin University beat UL Bohemians from Limerick 23-22. The winning score was a dropped goal by a French student at Trinity, Pierre Lazies, which he accomplished with the last kick of the game.

In all the circumstances, it was a just end to the season for the winners. Dublin University, or, more familiarly, Trinity College, were celebrating their 150th anniversary this past season and are the oldest club in continuous existence in world rugby, founded back in 1854.

The third division final resulted in an 18-11 win for Greystones over Ards. But the big winners on the day were Shannon, who since the play-offs were introduced in 1997-98 have appeared in six of these matches and have won on all six occasions.

France: Agony to Ecstasy for Stade

by CHRIS THAU

'Evidently the post-mortem of the Béziers disaster had such an impact that a week later Stade Français ignited, producing a clinical performance of ferocious, relentless rugby ...'

The gallant efforts of the French champions, Stade Français, to emerge from the depths of their miserable early-season woes, when they were knocked out of the Heineken Cup and had to wait until 19 December for their first win in the Top 16 championship, were duly rewarded with a momentous finale at Stade de France – a genuine journey from agony to ecstasy. The virtue of the departed South African coach, Nick Mallett, was that he did not lose his head and press the panic button as form slumped and the results seem to sink from bad to worse. His business-as-usual approach, supported, to his eternal credit, by club owner Max Guazzini, paid off in the end as the Parisians sailed through the final against Perpignan with confidence and panache to win their second consecutive title, the twelfth in their history.

It has to be understood that Stade Français – one of the oldest French clubs, having won the French Championship for the first time in 1893, the second time the Bouclier de Brennus was on offer – are not your ordinary club. The team is a Parisian outfit, a cosmopolitan gathering of aspiring stars and established celebrities, similar to England's Harlequins, the metropolitan club all provincial outfits love to hate. They recruit high-profile coaches and players, who bring to the club not only expertise but also glamour. The players, many of them seasoned internationals with a remarkable pedigree, hold the balance of power, with coaches recruited to service the team, not the other way around. But this is Paris, where appearance sometimes takes priority over substance, and player power is a fact of life.

The June 2004 climax at Stade de France was not only a fitting final act for French-speaking former Springbok Nick Mallett, who officially left Paris for his native South Africa for family reasons; it also provided a grand exit for the darling of the crowds, fly half Diego Dominguez, the charismatic Argentinian-born player who became a celebrity under the flag of Italy. Dominguez, who retired from international rugby and resisted calls from the Italian Federation to return for RWC 2003, had agreed with Guazzini to carry on for another season to enable the young and talented David Skrela to settle in and make the transition from hopeful to seasoned playmaker. The success of this enterprise was illustrated in the final, in which Dominguez – as the crowd chanted his name – produced a perfect seven out of seven until replaced by Skrela after 55 minutes. Stade were leading 28-6, and Dominguez was responsible for 20 of these 28 with five penalties, a dropped goal and a conversion (the remaining eight points were scored by Christophe Dominici with his first successful dropped goal of the year and Mauro Bergamasco at the end of a tumultuous forward charge). Dominguez has entered Stade Français folklore, but more significantly his faultless display is likely to land him the plum job of coaching the kickers of the French national team.

However, as is the way nowadays, any club targeting the French League title had, one way or another, to cross swords with Toulouse, either in the final, as Stade Français had done the year before, or in the knock-out stages of the play-offs, as the Parisians had to do this year. The turning point for Stade Français' glorious end of season was their comprehensive 25-12 three-tries-to-none defeat at the hands of Béziers in the play-offs, which left them with only one avenue open to the final – to defeat Toulouse in the last play-off the following weekend. Evidently the post-mortem of the Béziers disaster had such an impact that a week later Stade Français ignited, producing a clinical performance of ferocious, relentless rugby to annihilate their arch-rivals 49-17. The ruthlessness of the seven-try demolition at the Jean-Bouin Stadium in Paris reminded one of Toulouse's own proud reaction when questions about their ability, courage and commitment are posed.

The overwhelming defeat seemingly dealt the battered and bruised Toulouse such a psychological blow that they simply were unable to recover in time for the semi-final against Perpignan, which they narrowly lost 18-16 in Montpellier. In fairness, Perpignan have been going from strength to strength this season, and their success story has yet to be fully told. Their young team is the one to watch this year, in both Europe and France, where the Top 16 consists of a single pool for the first time, as they have both the firepower and the rugby expertise to go all the way.

The post-mortem of the Stade Français against Stade Toulousain match rumbled on long after the end of the championship, with the media trying to analyse the causes of the Toulouse failure against the reasons for the success of Stade Français. One of the most credible analyses singled out the early exit from the Heineken Cup of an exhausted Stade Français, with their large band of tired internationals returning from RWC 2003 duty, as the cause for their fresher and more successful end of season. Toulouse, on the other hand, finished empty-handed having chased both trophies until the very end.

In their semi, Stade Français could not put a foot wrong, seeing off Bourgoin 31-21 in Lyon, in a match more memorable for the presence of 35,000 people and the unexpected achievement of Bourgoin in having reached the semi-finals than for any spectacular feats of rugby football. After all that, there was very little Perpignan could do in the final to stop the relentless march of Stade towards the coveted shield. The southern side went down 38-20, and the 105th French Championship title went to Paris.

Elsewhere, the end of the season is remembered for the outburst of a frustrated Toulouse president René Bouscatel, who rudely interrupted France team manager Jo Maso, as he was reading the names of the French players selected for the North American tour, by calling the FFR and its staff 'liars' to the embarrassed amusement of the media and the players. After the tour, when the Toulouse and France captain, Fabien Pelous, was asked to comment on the trip in view of his club president's outburst, he was in diplomatic mode, describing the tour as 'a very useful venture for identifying talent for the future'.

BELOW Stade legend Diego Dominguez produced another masterful performance – seven goals from seven attempts – before taking his final bow after 55 minutes of the French Championship final v Perpignan.

Italy: Treviso Rule the Roost

by CHRIS THAU

'Indeed, in his first year … Treviso won the league, and soon after [Craig] Green delivered the second consecutive title it was confirmed that he would be in charge again next season.'

As his club was progressing relentlessly towards its eleventh championship title in the final with Ghial Amatori Calvisano in Padua on 19 June, Benetton Treviso president Amerino Zatta must have congratulated himself on the quality of his foreign recruits. His 26-year-old Australian left wing Brendan Williams kept scoring try after try, while full back Simon Mason, born 30 years ago in England, kept the scoreboard ticking with his accurate place-kicking. In the end Benetton won 22-11, with Williams scoring a hat-trick of tries – he ended as the top try scorer in the Italian Premiership – and Mason banging over two conversions and a penalty to finish second in the Super 10 points-scoring table with 222 points behind Calvisano's Gerard Fraser, the author of 239.

This was Benetton's second consecutive league (Super 10) title and their third in four years, with Calvisano, the seemingly eternal runners-up, once again doing a vanishing act at the last hurdle – their fourth failed attempt to capture the *scudetto* (championship) in four years. They failed in both 2001 and 2002 under New Zealander Craig Green and failed again under French coach Gilbert Doucet last year and in 2004. However, to diminish Calvisano's mounting disappointment, the club won the FIR Cup, beating Arix Viadana 21-8 in the final.

Green, a leading member of the 1987 All Black World Cup-winning team, moved to Treviso after three frustrating years with Calvisano, who had inherited the playing assets, but not the

championship-winning edge, of Amatori Milano when the Milanese club folded in 1998. Treviso, the heartland of Veneto rugby, had superb facilities sponsored by the Benetton Foundation and more significantly a big – by Italian standards anyway – budget.

Indeed, in his first year with his new club, Treviso won the league, and soon after Green delivered the second consecutive title it was confirmed that he would be in charge again next season. A different fate was awaiting his Calvisano successor, Frenchman Gilbert Doucet, a former flank forward with Toulon during their 1980s heyday, who before taking up the poisoned chalice of Calvisano had coached Grenoble in France and then Roma Olimpic for four years.

A terse statement said that Doucet left Calvisano by mutual consent – whatever that may mean in professional rugby. He is going to be replaced by former scrum half Andrea Cavinato, the coach of Italy Under 21, a man valued by national coach John Kirwan for his relentless passion, tactical acumen and eye for talent. Cavinato, born in Treviso 41 years ago, played briefly for the club during the 1980s before settling in Casale, where he finished his playing career.

Musical chairs are at their dizziest during the summer, as coaching contracts are renegotiated, or terminated, by mutual consent or not. In Parma, the only city to boast two Super 10 rugby clubs, local boy Stefano Romagnoli is leaving GrAN Parma for Viadana's greener pastures, while another local hero, former Italy scrum half Alessandro Ghini, is staying put at Overmach, having replaced South Africa's Dawie Snyman the year before. Meanwhile, 50-year-old Alejandro Canale, born in Cordoba, Argentina, is moving back to Rovigo after a year with Silea, while another frustrated coach, Frenchman Jean-Michel Vuillemin, is leaving the once great club of L'Aquila for the newly promoted Amatori Catania, in Sicily, where he hopes that he will be able to match the ambition of the Sicilians with the funds made available for player recruitment. After defeating Piacenza in the play-offs of the first division and leading his old club back to the Super 10, the former player-coach and manager of Catania, international flank forward Orazio Arancio, is concentrating on management duties and on his increasingly influential role within the Italian Federation Executive.

L'Aquila, meanwhile, have acquired the services of former Mirano coach Marzio Zanato (the first Venetian to coach the Abruzzi club), who had a very good season with Rovigo last year. Brescia's leading club, Leonessa 1928, survived in the top ten after the previous year's promotion, but as their two coaches, Frank Bunce and Matthew Vaea, left for New Zealand, the club have signed the very experienced Lyn Howells, made redundant by the collapse of the Celtic Warriors franchise in Wales. Should Howells overcome the language barrier – although English is very much lingua franca at the Italian club – and should the club's president-owner, Diego Rivetti, put more money into the recruitment pot, the ambitious northern Italian club may emulate the feat of the 1975 generation, who won the Italian League under the more modest name of Rugby Brescia.

The once undisputed leaders of the Italian club scene, APS Petrarca Padova, have parted company with Italo-Argentinian Rodolfo Ambrosio and gone for the services of Frenchman Philippe Sauton, made redundant by the Romanian Federation after a comparatively unsuccessful season as national coach. Petrarca – 11 times champions between 1969 and 1987 – are sponsored by the local Jesuit society and the Padua municipality and are the only club in Italy to match the facilities of Treviso. And after 13 years in the premier league and a championship title in 2000, Rugby Roma Olimpic have been relegated to the second division, leaving the Italian capital without a representative in the elite section of the league. There are now five Roman clubs in the first division, of which, reckon the observers, Massimo Mascioletti's Capitolina are most likely to go up.

Meanwhile it has been confirmed that John Kirwan will coach Italy until after RWC 2007, a logical and welcome decision by FIR president Giancarlo Dondi. Former Wallaby Tim Lane, who has coached extensively in France and South Africa, has joined Kirwan as an assistant, a very valuable signing indeed as Italy build up for 2007. Kirwan confirmed Grant Doorey as defensive coach and Carlo Orlandi as forward coach, areas in which the Italian game has improved in leaps and bounds. Another valuable addition to the management team is Carlo Checchinato, who decided to call it a day after four World Cups and 83 caps. He has been appointed assistant manager to Marco Bollesan, a sound operator who captained and coached Italy before he was appointed manager in 2002.

LEFT Benetton Treviso's prolific try scoring wing Brendan Williams (right) in defensive mode against his Bourgoin opposite number Kevin Zhakata in the 2003-04 Heineken Cup.

A Summary of the Season 2003-04

by BILL MITCHELL

RUGBY WORLD CUP 2003

POOL A

Australia	24	Argentina	8
Ireland	45	Romania	17
Argentina	67	Namibia	14
Australia	90	Romania	8
Ireland	64	Namibia	7
Argentina	50	Romania	3
Australia	142	Namibia	0
Argentina	15	Ireland	16
Namibia	7	Romania	37
Australia	17	Ireland	16

	W	D	L	F	A	BP	Pts
Australia	4	0	0	273	32	2	18
Ireland	3	0	1	141	56	3	15
Argentina	2	0	2	140	57	3	11
Romania	1	0	3	65	192	1	5
Namibia	0	0	4	28	310	0	0

POOL B

France	81	Fiji	18
Scotland	32	Japan	11
Fiji	19	United States	18
France	51	Japan	29
Scotland	39	United States	15
Fiji	41	Japan	13
France	51	Scotland	9
Japan	26	United States	39
France	41	United States	14
Scotland	22	Fiji	20

	W	D	L	F	A	BP	Pts
France	4	0	0	204	70	4	20
Scotland	3	0	1	102	97	2	14
Fiji	2	0	2	98	114	2	10
United States	1	0	3	86	125	2	6
Japan	0	0	4	79	163	0	0

POOL C

South Africa	72	Uruguay	6
Engand	84	Georgia	13
Samoa	60	Uruguay	13
South Africa	6	England	25
Georgia	9	Samoa	46
South Africa	46	Georgia	19
England	35	Samoa	22
Georgia	12	Uruguay	24
South Africa	60	Samoa	10
England	111	Uruguay	13

	W	D	L	F	A	BP	Pts
England	4	0	0	255	47	3	19
South Africa	3	0	1	184	60	3	15
Samoa	2	0	2	138	117	2	10
Uruguay	1	0	3	56	255	0	4
Georgia	0	0	4	46	200	0	0

POOL D

New Zealand	70	Italy	7
Wales	41	Canada	10
Italy	36	Tonga	12
New Zealand	68	Canada	6
Wales	27	Tonga	20
Italy	19	Canada	14
New Zealand	91	Tonga	7
Italy	15	Wales	27
Canada	24	Tonga	7
New Zealand	53	Wales	37

	W	D	L	F	A	BP	Pts
New Zealand	4	0	0	282	57	4	20
Wales	3	0	1	132	98	2	14
Italy	2	0	2	77	123	0	8
Canada	1	0	3	54	135	1	5
Tonga	0	0	4	46	178	1	1

KNOCK-OUT STAGES

Quarter-finals

New Zealand	29	South Africa	9
Australia	33	Scotland	16
France	43	Ireland	21
England	28	Wales	17

Semi-finals

Australia	22	New Zealand	10
England	24	France	7

Third-place Play-off

New Zealand	40	France	13

Final

Australia	17	England	20

(after extra time)

INTERNATIONAL RUGBY

ENGLAND TO NEW ZEALAND & AUSTRALIA JUNE 2004

Opponents	Results
NEW ZEALAND	L 3-36
NEW ZEALAND	L 12-36
AUSTRALIA	L 15-51

Played 3 Lost 3

IRELAND TO SOUTH AFRICA JUNE 2004

Opponents	Results
SOUTH AFRICA	L 17-31
SOUTH AFRICA	L 17-26

Played 2 Lost 2

SCOTLAND TO SOUTHERN HEMISPHERE JUNE 2004

Opponents	Results
Queensland	L 5-41
New South Wales Country	W 48-10
SAMOA	W 38-3
New South Wales Waratahs	L 15-33
AUSTRALIA	L 15-35
AUSTRALIA	L 13-34

Played 6 Won 2 Lost 4

WALES TO ARGENTINA & SOUTH AFRICA JUNE 2004

Opponents	Results
ARGENTINA	L 44-50
ARGENTINA	W 35-20
SOUTH AFRICA	L 18-53

Played 3 Won 1 Lost 2

CHURCHILL CUP 2004

Semi-finals

New Zealand Maori	69	United States	31
Canada	23	England A	48

Consolation

Canada	32	United States	29

Final

England A	19	New Zealand Maori	26

(after extra time)

ROYAL BANK OF SCOTLAND SIX NATIONS CHAMPIONSHIP 2004

Results

France	35	Ireland	17
Wales	23	Scotland	10
Italy	9	England	50
France	25	Italy	0
Ireland	36	Wales	15
Scotland	13	England	35
Italy	20	Scotland	15
England	13	Ireland	19
Wales	22	France	29
Ireland	19	Italy	3
England	31	Wales	21
Scotland	0	France	31
Wales	45	Italy	10
Ireland	37	Scotland	16
France	24	England	21

Final table

	P	W	D	L	F	A	Pts
France	5	5	0	0	144	60	10
Ireland	5	4	0	1	128	82	8
England	5	3	0	2	150	86	6
Wales	5	2	0	3	125	116	4
Italy	5	1	0	4	42	152	2
Scotland	5	0	0	5	53	146	0

France win the Grand Slam, Ireland the Triple Crown

WORLD CUP WARM-UP MATCHES

Results

Ireland	35	Wales	12
France	56	Romania	8
Wales	9	England	43
France	17	England	16
England	45	France	14
Scotland	47	Italy	15
Scotland	10	Ireland	29
Wales	23	Scotland	9
Ireland	61	Italy	6
Wales	54	Romania	8
Italy	31	Georgia	22

OTHER INTERNATIONAL MATCHES

Results

Pacific Islands	24	South Africa	38
Australia	29	Pacific Islands	14
United States	31	France	39
Japan	19	Italy	32
New Zealand	41	Pacific Islands	26
Canada	13	France	47
New Zealand	41	Argentina	7
Romania	25	Italy	24
England XV	42	NZ Barbarians	17
France A	27	England A	22

SIX NATIONS UNDER 21 CHAMPIONSHIP 2004

Results

France	20	Ireland	20
Italy	3	England	57
Wales	39	Scotland	16
Ireland	30	Wales	19
Scotland	9	England	27
France	46	Italy	21
England	27	Ireland	19
Italy	38	Scotland	41
Wales	9	France	36
England	22	Wales	19
Ireland	33	Italy	0
Scotland	14	France	36
France	18	England	25
Ireland	33	Scotland	9
Wales	49	Italy	17

Sporting Index
World Leaders in Sports Spread Betting

OUR LIGHT IS ALWAYS ON

24/7 phone betting. Something no other sports spread betting firm offers.

sportingindex.com   08000 96 96 45   24hr phone trading   ch4 text p604   just press●

make your passion pay!

	P	W	D	L	F	A	Pts
England	5	5	0	0	158	68	10
France	5	3	1	1	156	89	7
Ireland	5	3	1	1	135	75	7
Wales	5	2	0	3	135	121	4
Scotland	5	1	0	4	89	173	2
Italy	5	0	0	5	79	226	0

UNDER 21 WORLD CHAMPIONSHIP 2004

(Held in June in Scotland)

Eleventh-place Play-off
Russia 44 Tonga 39

Ninth-place Play-off
Italy 27 Scotland 16

Seventh-place Play-off
Argentina 42 France 33

Fifth-place Play-off
England 26 Wales 19

Semi-finals
Ireland 26 Australia 13
New Zealand 26 South Africa 11

Third-place Play-off
South Africa 44 Australia 10

Final
New Zealand 47 Ireland 19

OTHER UNDER 21 INTERNATIONAL

Result
Scotland 26 Ireland 27

UNDER 19 WORLD CHAMPIONSHIP 2004

(Held in March and April in South Africa)

Ninth-place Play-off
Argentina 58 Italy 3

Seventh-place Play-off
Japan 28 Scotland 22

Fifth-place Play-off
Wales 14 Australia 10

Semi-finals
France 18 England 12
New Zealand 30 South Africa 23

Third-place Play-off
South Africa 38 England 31

Final
New Zealand 34 France 12

Ireland withdrew due to the death of a player

OTHER AGE-GROUP MATCH

Result
Scotland U19 6 Wales Schools 3

UNDER 18 HOME INTERNATIONALS

(Held in April in Belfast)

Results
Ireland 12 England 15
Scotland 0 Wales 36
Scotland 10 England 16
Ireland 11 Wales 22
Ireland 3 Scotland 14
England 11 Wales 29

Final table

	P	W	D	L	F	A	Pts
Wales	3	3	0	0	87	22	6
England	3	2	0	1	42	51	4
Scotland	3	1	0	2	24	55	2
Ireland	3	0	0	3	26	51	0

Title retained by Wales

YOUTH MATCHES

Results
Scotland 15 France 12
Italy 15 Scotland 29
Italy 0 Scotland 15

IRB SEVENS SERIES FINALS 2003-04

Dubai
South Africa 33 New Zealand 26

South Africa (George)
England 38 New Zealand 14

New Zealand (Wellington)
New Zealand 33 Fiji 15

United States (Carson, California)
Argentina 21 New Zealand 12

Singapore
South Africa 24 Argentina 19

Hong Kong
England 22 Argentina 12

France (Bordeaux)
New Zealand 28 England 19

England (Twickenham)
England 22 New Zealand 19

New Zealand (128 points) win the IRB World Sevens Series; 2nd: England (122); 3rd: Argentina (86).

TRI-NATIONS 2004

Results

New Zealand	16	Australia	7
New Zealand	23	South Africa	21
Australia	30	South Africa	26
Australia	23	New Zealand	18
South Africa	40	New Zealand	26
South Africa	23	Australia	19

South Africa win Tri-Nations 2004

WOMEN'S CHURCHILL CUP 2004

Semi-finals

Canada	11	England	39
United States	0	New Zealand	35

Consolation

Canada	10	United States	29

Final

New Zealand	38	England	0

WOMEN'S SIX NATIONS

Results

France	22	Ireland	5
Spain	8	Ireland	7
Wales	15	Scotland	30
Spain	3	England	71
Scotland	7	England	20
Ireland	13	Wales	14
France	24	Spain	0
England	51	Ireland	10
Spain	6	Scotland	5
Wales	0	France	22
England	53	Wales	3
Scotland	12	France	16
France	13	England	12
Ireland	0	Scotland	17
Wales	7	Spain	12

Final table

	P	W	D	L	F	A	Pts
France	5	5	0	0	97	29	10
England	5	4	0	1	207	36	8
Spain	5	3	0	2	29	114	6
Scotland	5	2	0	3	71	57	4
Wales	5	1	0	4	39	130	2
Ireland	5	0	0	5	35	112	0

OTHER WOMEN'S INTERNATIONALS

Results

France	8	England	6
Scotland	11	Wales	10
South Africa	15	Wales	16

CLUB, COUNTY AND DIVISIONAL RUGBY

ENGLAND

Powergen Cup
Quarter-finals

Leeds	21	Bath	10
Sale	26	Saracens	6
Newcastle	24	London Irish	12
Wasps	24	Pertemps Bees	28

Semi-finals

Sale	33	Leeds	20
Newcastle	53	Pertemps Bees	3

Final

Newcastle	37	Sale	33

Zurich Premiership

	P	W	D	L	F	A	BP	Pts
Bath	22	18	0	4	208	211	7	79
Wasps	22	16	0	6	575	406	9	72
Northampton	22	15	1	6	536	416	8	70
Gloucester	22	14	0	8	489	412	7	63
Leicester	22	11	3	6	537	430	6	55*
Harlequins	22	10	2	10	502	449	10	54
Sale	22	9	3	10	510	470	11	53
London Irish	22	10	1	11	427	454	7	49
Newcastle	22	7	2	13	497	525	11	43
Saracens	22	8	1	13	397	541	6	39*
Leeds	22	7	1	14	449	586	7	37
Rotherham	22	0	0	22	309	779	3	3

*Denotes point deducted for fielding an ineligible player

Zurich Premiership Play-offs
Semi-final

Wasps	57	Northampton	20

Final

Wasps	10	Bath	6

Wildcard Final

Leicester	48	Sale	27

National Leagues
1st Division Champions: Worcester
Runners-up: Orrell
2nd Division Champions: Sedgley Park
Runners-up: Nottingham
3rd Division North Champions: Halifax
Runners-up: Waterloo
3rd Division South Champions: Blackheath
Runners-up: Launceston

Powergen Challenge Shield Final

Bristol	53	Waterloo	24

Powergen Intermediate Cup Final

Bradford and Bingley	46	Gloucester OB	18

Powergen Junior Vase Final

Leodiensian	13	North Ribblesdale	13

(Leodiensian win on 2-1 try count)

Tetley's Bitter County Championship Final

Devon	43	Gloucestershire	14

Tetley's Bitter County Shield Final

North Midlands	58	Eastern Counties	5

University Match

Oxford U	11	Cambridge U	11

University Second Teams Match

OU Greyhounds	44	CU LX Club	19

University U21 Match

Oxford U	22	Cambridge U	0

Other University U21 Match

CU U21 A	9	OU U21 A	12

Women's University Match

Oxford U	10	Cambridge U	7

Women's University Second Teams Match

Cambridge U	0	Oxford U	10

British Universities Sports Association
Men's Final

Durham U	31	Exeter U	24

Women's Final

Loughborough U	17	UWIC (Cardiff Inst)	7

Hospitals Cup Winners: Imperial Medicals
Inter-Services Champions: The Army

Middlesex Sevens Winners: Northampton Saints
Middlesex Sevens Plate Winners: Gloucester

Rosslyn Park National Schools Sevens (*sponsored by Wooden Spoon*)
Festival Winners: Cheltenham College
Colts Winners: Millfield School
Junior Winners: QEGS Wakefield
Preparatory School Winners: St Olave's School
Girls Schools Winners: Wycombe Abbey School
Open Winners: Ivybridge School

Daily Mail Schools Day (at Twickenham)
Under 18 Cup Winners: Colston's School, Bristol
Under 18 Vase Winners: St Benedict's School, Whitehaven
Under 15 Cup Winners: John Cleveland School, Rugby

Women's National Cup Final

Saracens	10	Wasps	8

Women's Division One Champions: Wasps
Women's Division One Runners-up: Clifton

ARE PROUD TO SUPPORT

WOODEN SPOON RUGBY WORLD '05

SCOTLAND

BT Cup Final
Glasgow Hawks   29   Dundee HSFP   17
BT Shield Final
Berwick   42   Glasgow Acads   24
BT Bowl Final
Perthshire   18   Hawick YM   6

Scottish Sevens Winners
Kelso: Gala
Selkirk: Rotherham
Gala: Royal Scots
Melrose: Stellenbosch University
Hawick: Watsonians
Berwick: Gala
Langholm: Hawick
Earlston: Gala
Jed-Forest: Watsonians
Kings of Sevens title: Gala

BT Scotland Premiership
Division One

	P	W	D	L	F	A	BP	Pts
Glasgow Hawks	22	20	1	1	567	278	8	90
Boroughmuir	22	15	0	7	713	629	18	78
Aberdeen GSFP	22	13	3	6	603	508	14	72
Watsonians	22	12	0	10	540	502	11	59
Heriot's RFC	22	12	1	9	496	499	8	58
Melrose	22	11	1	10	448	492	6	46
Hawick	22	10	0	12	452	522	6	46
Currie	22	8	1	13	423	536	9	43
Glasgow HA	22	7	0	15	455	480	13	41
Ayr	22	9	1	12	377	504	3	41
Stirling County	22	7	0	15	487	564	10	38
Peebles	22	3	2	17	424	673	9	25

Champions: Glasgow Hawks
Relegated: Peebles, Stirling County

Division Two

	P	W	D	L	F	A	BP	Pts
Gala	22	18	0	4	602	270	13	85
Biggar	22	16	2	4	714	252	16	84
Dundee HSFP	22	15	1	6	669	308	19	81
Stewart's-Melville	22	13	1	8	541	422	14	68
Kelso	22	14	0	8	502	393	8	64
Haddington	22	13	1	8	463	422	8	62
Jed-Forest	22	10	1	11	462	407	12	54
Selkirk	22	8	0	14	389	501	10	42
Murrayfield W	22	8	1	13	343	584	2	36
Kirkcaldy	22	6	0	14	352	586	9	33
Grangemouth	22	4	1	17	289	640	3	21
West of Scotland	22	3	0	19	276	658	6	18

Promoted: Gala (Champions), Biggar
Relegated: Grangemouth, West of Scotland

Division Three
Champions: Edinburgh Academicals
Runners-up: Berwick

WALES

Konica Minolta Cup
Quarter-finals
Brynmawr   3   Bridgend   17
Caerphilly   29   Swansea   21
Cross Keys   21   Aberavon   38
Neath   27   Pontypridd   18
Semi-finals
Aberavon   22   Caerphilly   33
Bridgend   14   Neath   29
Final
Neath   36   Caerphilly   13

Welsh Premier Division

	P	W	D	L	F	A	Ts	Pts
Newport	30	27	1	2	1054	150	142	82
Neath	30	23	1	6	947	557	114	70
Pontypridd	30	20	2	8	820	641	92	62
Aberavon	30	17	0	13	774	627	93	51
Carmarthen Qns	30	16	1	13	674	629	76	49
Swansea	30	16	0	14	853	710	96	48
Bridgend	30	14	1	15	757	767	93	43
Cross Keys	30	13	0	17	753	777	83	39
Bedwas	30	12	2	16	644	797	72	38
Caerphilly	30	11	1	18	658	918	82	34
Pontypool	30	11	1	18	543	698	59	34
Cardiff	30	11	0	19	649	797	87	33
Newbridge	30	10	3	17	545	803	78	33
Llanelli	30	10	2	18	701	765	86	32
Llandovery	30	19	2	18	681	787	82	32
Ebbw Vale	30	10	1	19	554	824	58	31

Lloyds TSB Welsh Leagues
Division One

	P	W	D	L	F	A	Pts
Llanharan	30	28	1	1	1361	197	85
Maesteg	30	27	1	2	1336	326	82
Whitland	30	23	0	7	970	465	69
Narberth	30	22	0	8	1978	527	66
Brynmawr	30	20	0	10	790	610	60
Llangennech	30	18	1	11	788	561	55
Carmarthen Ath	30	18	0	12	890	736	54
Beddau	30	14	1	15	797	567	43
Glamorgan W	30	14	1	15	714	658	43
Bonymaen	30	13	1	16	672	706	40
Blackwood	30	11	2	17	632	672	35
UWIC (Card Inst)	30	11	1	18	684	810	34
Rumney	30	8	1	21	684	938	25
Tredegar	30	5	0	25	436	1175	15
Treorchy	30	3	0	27	347	1539	9
Tondu	30	0	0	30	218	1744	0

Relegated: Tondu, Treorchy, Tredegar, Rumney

Division Two East Champions: Builth Wells
Runners-up: Fleur de Lys
Division Two West Champions: Tonmawr
Runners-up: Bridgend Athletic
Division Three Champions
East: Brynithel
South East: Treherbert
South West: Banwen
West: Pontyberem

IRELAND

AIB League
Division One

	P	W	D	L	F	A	BP	Pts
Cork Constitution	14	11	1	2	287	251	5	51
Shannon	14	11	0	3	366	199	5	49
Belfast H'quins	14	10	0	4	361	219	8	48
Buccaneers	14	10	1	3	315	193	6	48
Ballymena	14	8	1	5	249	186	7	41
Blackrock College	14	9	0	5	257	236	4	40
Garryowen	14	8	1	5	260	286	3	37
County Carlow	14	5	1	8	304	282	10	32
Clontarf	14	5	1	8	251	243	9	31
UC Dublin	14	5	1	8	226	294	5	27
Lansdowne	14	4	1	9	251	305	4	22
Dungannon	14	4	0	10	185	249	4	20
Galwegians	14	4	0	10	213	355	4	20
St Mary's College	14	3	1	10	212	316	5	19
Dolphin	14	3	1	10	227	350	4	18

Semi-finals

Cork Constitution	20	Buccaneers	6
Shannon	27	Belfast Harlequins	12

Final

Shannon	22	Cork Constitution	16

Relegated: Dolphin, St Mary's College

Division Two

	P	W	D	L	F	A	BP	Pts
Dublin University	15	11	0	4	278	184	5	49
UL Bohemian	15	9	2	4	338	191	7	47
Univ College Cork	15	10	2	3	298	231	3	47
Old Belvedere	15	10	0	5	286	225	7	47
Bective Rangers	15	10	2	3	242	193	3	47
De la Salle-P'ton	15	9	1	5	265	206	6	44
Old Crescent	15	8	1	6	256	236	5	39
Barnhall	15	8	0	7	252	199	6	38
Terenure College	15	7	0	8	221	270	4	32
Ballynahinch	15	5	3	7	225	262	4	30
Malone	15	5	0	10	253	299	8	28
Thomond	15	5	0	10	227	256	7	27
Midleton	15	5	1	9	175	223	5	27
Waterpark	15	3	2	10	236	287	8	24
Young Munster	15	5	0	10	208	310	4	24
Sundays Well	15	3	0	12	214	402	6	18

Promoted: Dublin University
Relegated: Sundays Well

CELTIC CUP

Semi-finals

Connacht	25	Edinburgh	26
Glasgow	13	Ulster	20

Final

Ulster	27	Edinburgh	21

CELTIC LEAGUE

	P	W	D	L	F	A	BP	Pts
Llanelli Scarlets	22	16	1	5	597	385	10	76
Ulster	22	15	0	7	617	363	12	72
Gwent Dragons	22	16	0	6	590	449	8	72
Celtic Warriors	22	14	0	8	560	451	9	65
Neath-S'sea Osp	22	11	1	10	582	512	9	55
Cardiff Blues	22	11	0	11	570	467	10	54
Munster	22	10	0	12	422	456	11	51
Leinster	22	9	1	12	523	580	9	47
Connacht	22	8	2	12	479	550	8	44
Edinburgh	22	9	0	13	454	622	8	44
Glasgow	22	6	1	15	442	614	6	32
Borders	22	4	0	18	363	750	6	22

FRANCE

French Championship

Pool A

	P	W	D	L	F	A	Pts
Perpignan	6	5	0	1	169	75	16
Bourgoin	6	3	0	3	147	137	12
Castres	6	3	0	3	143	126	12
Béziers	6	1	0	5	76	184	8

Pool B

	P	W	D	L	F	A	Pts
Stade Français	6	4	0	2	151	100	14
Toulouse	6	4	0	2	136	133	14
Biarritz	6	3	0	3	149	107	12
Brive	6	1	0	5	82	178	8

Semi-finals

Perpignan	18	Toulouse	16
Stade Français	31	Bourgoin	21

Final

Stade Français	38	Perpignan	20

ITALY

Italian Championship

Final

Benetton Treviso	22	Calvisano	11

NEW ZEALAND

National Provincial Championship

Final

Wellington	29	Auckland	41

Ranfurly Shield holders: Auckland

AUSTRALIA

Leading State: ACT Brumbies

SOUTH AFRICA

Currie Cup 2003

Final
Northern Blue Bulls   40   Natal Sharks   19

BARBARIANS

Opponents	Results
Combined Services	W 26-8
Leicester	L 21-69
East Midlands	W 104-10
SCOTLAND	W 40-33
WALES	L 0-42
ENGLAND	W 32-12
PORTUGAL	W 66-35

Played 7, Won 5, Lost 2

SUPER 12 TOURNAMENT 2004

Final table

	P	W	D	L	F	A	Pts
Brumbies	11	8	0	3	406	269	40
Crusaders	11	7	0	4	345	303	34
Stormers	11	7	0	4	286	260	33
Chiefs	11	7	0	4	274	251	33
Blues	11	6	1	4	337	309	32
Blue Bulls	11	6	1	5	302	320	28
Sharks	11	5	0	6	267	305	28
Waratahs	11	5	0	6	342	274	27
Highlanders	11	4	1	6	299	347	26
Reds	11	5	0	6	217	240	25
Hurricanes	11	4	1	6	276	309	23
Cats	11	1	0	10	294	459	11

Semi-finals
Brumbies   32   Chiefs   17
Crusaders   27   Stormers   16

Final
Brumbies   47   Crusaders   38

HEINEKEN CUP

Quarter-finals
Llanelli   10   Biarritz   27
Munster   37   Stade Français   32
Toulouse   36   Edinburgh   10
Wasps   34   Gloucester   3

Semi-finals
Munster   32   Wasps   37
Toulouse   19   Biarritz   11

Final
Wasps   27   Toulouse   20

PARKER PEN CHALLENGE CUP

Semi-finals
Bath   29   Montferrand   15
Montferrand   38   Bath   22
(aggregate 53-51)

Harlequins   31   Connacht   22
Connacht   23   Harlequins   18
(aggregate 49-45)

Final
Harlequins   27   Montferrand   26

PARKER PEN SHIELD

Semi-finals
Montpellier   45   Leonessa   12
Leonessa   23   Montpellier   26
(aggregate 71-35)

Rugby Parma   32   Viadana   42
Viadana   33   Rugby Parma   27
(aggregate 75-59)

Final
Montpellier   25   Viadana   19

Submerge yourself into an unforgettable holiday.

Delta offers daily service from Manchester and London to the USA. Once in the US, we offer quick and hassle-free connections from our hubs to over 150 US cities. Special features include advanced seat reservations and special meal requests. For more information, log on to delta.com, call your local travel agent or us at 0800 414 767.

PREVIEW OF THE SEASON 2004-05

Key Players 2004-05

by IAN ROBERTSON

ENGLAND

MIKE TINDALL

At the age of 22, Mike Tindall had made such an impact at Bath in the Zurich Premiership that he was selected for his first cap for England in the centre against Scotland, and he celebrated by scoring a try. Although he has missed a few games through injury he has firmly established himself in the England team alongside Will Greenwood, and they have been one of the best centre partnerships in international rugby for the past three years. He had an excellent World Cup. A very powerful, direct runner in attack with plenty of pace, he is also an extremely aggressive, totally committed tackler in defence. He was unfortunately injured at the start of the 2004 Six Nations Championship, but he was back on duty for the Tests against New Zealand and Australia in the summer and is now one of the more experienced England backs. He looks sure to be chosen for the Lions tour to New Zealand in 2005, and he is likely to be England's first-choice centre for the long-term future.

JOE WORSLEY

The English back row has been one of the great strengths of the side during the past five years, and Lawrence Dallaglio, Richard Hill and Neil Back have set a record for the most appearances together at international level. During this period Joe Worsley spent a lot of time on the bench, but he did win a lot of caps as a replacement. He first played at Test level in the 1999 World Cup, and he appeared regularly throughout the next four seasons. He was first choice when Dallaglio was out through injury, and he was first choice in his own right for the 2004 Six Nations Championship and England's summer tour to New Zealand and Australia. He has the advantage of playing alongside Dallaglio at club level for Wasps, and he had a good season with England in 2004 even though the results dipped after the heady success of the World Cup. He has played his full part in England's well-organised defensive system and he is also a powerful, strong runner in attack. He is a leading contender for the British and Irish Lions tour to New Zealand.

SCOTLAND

CHRIS CUSITER

Scotland have produced a long line of very good scrum halves in the past 20 years, starting with Roy Laidlaw in the 1980s through to Bryan Redpath in the past five years via Gary Armstrong and Andy Nicol. A new name has suddenly exploded onto the international scene, with the arrival in 2004 for his first cap of Chris Cusiter at the age of just 21. He played his first Test in Wales and went on to play the rest of the Six Nations Championship and in the two Tests against Australia in the summer. He settled into the faster pace of international rugby virtually at once and has all the attributes of a top-class scrum half. He has a very quick pass and he also takes the pressure off his fly half with the ability to make breaks. He is all action throughout every game and he has a big appetite for defence. In the same way Jonny Wilkinson has set new standards for aggressive defence at fly half, Cusiter is on his way to becoming one of the best defensive scrum halves in the game. That is a bonus. He is a key player for Scotland because he does all the basic work of a scrum half to the highest levels and he looks like having a long career ahead of him.

SIMON TAYLOR

Following a wretched run of bad luck which has seen him suffer two very serious injuries, Simon Taylor will miss the first part of the 2004-05 season. One of the most talented forwards in world rugby, he appeared to have a great future ahead of him when he went on the Lions tour to Australia in 2001 after winning just a handful of caps for Scotland. Unfortunately he received a serious leg injury right at the beginning of the tour and he was out of rugby for several months. He recovered in time to play the whole of the 2002 and 2003 seasons for Scotland and he went to Australia in October 2003 for the World Cup, in which he emerged as one of the very best No. 8s in northern hemisphere rugby. Indeed, at the end of the World Cup he was voted the top No. 8 in the world after several outstanding performances. He began the Six Nations in 2004 in great form, but then he suffered another very bad injury which will keep him out of rugby until November. At 6ft 4ins and 17 stones, he is a formidable forward. He has great hands, is immensely strong and quick and is certain to make the 2005 Lions tour to New Zealand if fit.

WALES

GARETH THOMAS

Only just turned 30 years of age, Gareth Thomas is threequarters of the way to becoming the first Welsh player to win 100 caps for his country. That is a tribute not just to his longevity but also to his versatility. He has won his caps playing in three different positions in the back line – centre, wing and full back. He played in the 1995 World Cup in South Africa, where he won his first cap, and he celebrated by scoring three tries against Japan. He has been the most consistent back in the Welsh team for several years, and it is easy to see why he has been so successful. He has the power and strength to play in the centre, the speed to play on the wing and the all-round skills to flourish at full back. His ability to play in three different positions makes him pretty certain to go on the Lions tour to New Zealand in 2005, and before that he should play a major role in the continuing Welsh revival.

GARETH COOPER

It was never going to be easy to break into the full Welsh national team as long as Rob Howley continued to pursue his international career, but when he retired last year from the Welsh team to play only club rugby, Gareth Cooper was given his big break. He had played well at club level in the Zurich Premiership for Bath and played for Wales B before winning his first full cap against Italy in Rome in 2001. He has a quick service and is strong on the break. Since the retirement of Howley he has established himself in the Test team and he enjoyed a good World Cup in Australia. He has quickly struck up a good partnership with the Welsh fly half Stephen Jones, and largely through the skills of Cooper and Jones the Welsh backs have flourished in the past 18 months. Another good season in the Six Nations Championship and both Cooper and Jones are likely to make the Lions tour to New Zealand in 2005.

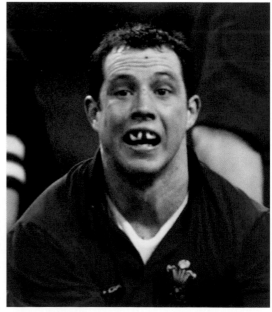

IRELAND

RONAN O'GARA

While most countries are very grateful if they can produce one top-quality international fly half, Ireland have the luxury of choosing between two – Ronan O'Gara and David Humphreys. When O'Gara won his first cap in 2000 against Scotland, Humphreys had already won 20, and in the past five seasons they have virtually shared 80 Irish caps between them. At the World Cup in Australia and through the 2004 Six Nations Championship O'Gara established himself as first-choice fly half, but Humphreys came on as a replacement in most of those games. O'Gara is arguably the more dangerous runner in attack and he is also very good at unleashing his back line. Like Humphreys, O'Gara is a prolific points scorer – he has topped 400 points in international rugby and is the second-highest scorer in Irish rugby behind his fly-half rival. He has struck up a tremendous partnership at half back with Peter Stringer for Munster and Ireland, and there is every likelihood that both will be chosen for the Lions tour to New Zealand, along with both centres – Brian O'Driscoll and Gordon D'Arcy – as well as most of the Irish pack.

MALCOLM O'KELLY

The Irish have arguably the best set of locks in the northern hemisphere, with three top-class players – Malcolm O'Kelly, Paul O'Connell and Donncha O'Callaghan. O'Kelly is far and away the longest-serving of those three as he won his first cap against the All Blacks in 1997. He has enjoyed a remarkable career as he was first capped at the age of 23, and even though he missed the 1999 Six Nations Championship through illness he still became the youngest Irish forward to gain 50 caps. He reached another big milestone when he won his sixty-fourth cap in March 2004, which took him past the record of 63 for an Irish lock forward set by the legendary Willie John McBride in the mid-1970s. He toured with the Lions to Australia in 2001 and is almost certain to go with the Lions to New Zealand in 2005. He had an outstanding World Cup in Australia in 2003 and he featured in at least two lists as one of the best two locks in the whole tournament alongside Martin Johnson of England. The Irish boast a terrific set of forwards, and O'Kelly is a key man in the engine room of the pack.

FRANCE

FREDERIC MICHALAK

The French have had a couple of pretty good fly halves recently in Christophe Lamaison and Gerald Merceron, but although they were good goal-kickers and steady players, neither was particularly dynamic in attack. Merceron made the occasional break, but he was more of a link man and a very good kicker. The French coach, Bernard Laporte, wanted his fly half to pose a threat in attack, and he decided to go for an inexperienced No. 10 who was almost ten years younger than Merceron. Michalak won his first cap two years ago when he was only 20 years of age, and had a rather shaky first two matches. He did make a big impression as an elusive runner, but he also made a lot of mistakes, and when he was selected for the World Cup there was a lot of pressure on him. He proved to be an excellent goal-kicker and had a very good tournament until the semi-final against England. He played really well in the French Grand Slam in the Six Nations in 2004 and he has the potential to be a great international fly half.

OLIVIER MAGNE

The top countries in the world all have had exceptionally good back rows in the past couple of years, and while England, Ireland, Australia and New Zealand would not swap their potential triumvirate for any other, the French firmly believe their trio of Olivier Magne, Imanol Harinordoquy and Serge Betsen are as good as any. While Harinordoquy is only 24 years of age, Magne and Betsen have both turned 30, so perhaps this French back row won't last more than another season or two. They are probably at their peak right now and they played a major role in helping France collect the Grand Slam in 2004 after all the disappointments at the World Cup in Australia in November 2003. That was the fourth French Grand Slam during the playing career of Magne and he has been the outstanding French forward in all of them, as well as in the 1999 and 2003 World Cups. A solid defensive player, he is the perfect all-round back-row forward and remains an inspiration to the French team.

ITALY

CRISTIAN STOICA

Although he was born in Bucharest and played his early rugby in Romania, Stoica has been a major influence on Italian rugby since he moved to Milan in 1996. With the retirement of Diego Dominguez, he is now the most capped player in the Italian threequarter line, having won his fiftieth cap in the World Cup in Australia. He is noted for being a very aggressive, powerful runner in attack and a tremendous tackler in defence. He is the ideal man to help the new Italy fly half settle into the helter-skelter world of international rugby, and his vast experience at the highest level has already helped the various relatively new players in the back division establish themselves in the team. The two brothers Manuel and Denis Dallan have both benefited hugely from playing alongside Stoica, and he is also likely to bring out the best in players like Andrea Masi, Rima Wakarua and Roland De Marigny. He is now at the height of his powers, but he is such an accomplished centre he could well be controlling back play through to the next World Cup.

MARCO BORTOLAMI

The Italian team have made steady progress since first joining the Six Nations Championship in 2000, and two victories against Scotland and one against Wales in the past five years have fully justified their inclusion in the tournament. They were, of course, blessed with that one-man points-scoring machine Diego Dominguez until 2003, and several other outstanding individuals have made notable contributions to their good performances. Their main problem at the highest level has been when their front five forwards have struggled against the very top teams like England, France and Scotland. After relying for years on the splendid lock forward Carlo Checchinato, Italy have produced another potential top-class second row – Marco Bortolami. At 6ft 5ins and 15½ stones, he has an imposing presence in the set pieces and he has the added bonus of being very lively in open play. Still in his early twenties he is the perfect player to build a useful pack around. A good line-out jumper and a solid scrummager, he is a key player for the future.

Fixtures 2004-05

AUGUST 2004

Sat, 14th	Middlesex Sevens (T'ham)
Sat, 21st	Kelso Sevens (prov)
Sat, 28th	English Senior Cup Qual Rd
	Scottish Premiership 1-3 (1)
	Welsh Challenge Cup Prelim Rd
Sun, 29th	Selkirk Sevens

SEPTEMBER 2004

Fri, 3rd/	
Sun, 5th	Celtic League (1)
Sat, 4th	Zurich Premiership (1)
	English Nat Leagues 1-3 (1)
	English Senior Cup Prelim Rd
	English Junior Cup Prelim Rd
	English Leagues (12 teams) (1)
	Scottish Premiership 1-3 (2)
	Scottish Nat Lges (all divs) (1)
	Welsh Lges Prem,1,2E,2W (1)
Fri, 10th/	
Sat, 11th	Celtic League (2)
Sat, 11th	Zurich Premiership (2)
	English Nat Leagues 1-3 (2)
	English Leagues (12 teams) (2)
	English Leagues (10 teams) (1)
	Scottish Premiership 1-3 (3)
	Scottish Nat Lges (all divs) (2)
	Welsh Lges Prem,1,2E,2W (2)
Wed, 15th	Welsh Lge Premier (3)
Fri, 17th/	
Sun, 19th	Celtic League (3)
Sat, 18th	Zurich Premiership (3)
	English Nat Leagues 1,2 (3)
	English Cups Rd 1
	Scottish Premiership 1-3 (4)
	Welsh Lge Premier (4)
	Welsh Lges 1,2E,2W (3)
Wed, 22nd	Welsh Lge 1 (4)
Fri, 24th/	
Sat, 25th	Celtic League (4)
Sat, 25th	Zurich Premiership (4)
	English Nat Leagues 1,2 (4)
	English Nat League 3 (3)
	English Leagues (12 teams) (3)
	English Leagues (10 teams) (2)
	Scottish Premiership 1-3 (5)
	Scottish Nat Lges (all divs) (3)
	Welsh Challenge Cup Rd 1
	Welsh Lges Premier,1 (5)
	Welsh Lges 2E,2W (4)
Wed, 29th	Welsh Lge Premier (6)

OCTOBER 2004

Fri, 1st/	
Sun, 3rd	Celtic League (5)
Sat, 2nd	Zurich Premiership (5)
	English Nat League 1 (5)

	English Leagues (12 teams) (4)
	English Leagues (10 teams) (3)
	English Senior Cup Rd 2
	Scottish Premiership 1-3 (6)
	Scottish Nat Lges (all divs) (4)
	Welsh Lge Premier (7)
	Welsh Lge 1 (6)
	Welsh Lges 2E,2W (5)
Wed, 6th	Welsh Lge 1 (7)
Fri, 8th/	
Sun, 10th	Celtic League (6)
Sat, 9th	Zurich Premiership (6)
	English Nat League 1 (6)
	English Nat League 2 (5)
	English Nat League 3 (4)
	English Leagues (12 teams) (5)
	English Leagues (10 teams) (4)
	Scottish Premiership 1-3 (7)
	Welsh Lges Premier,1 (8)
	Welsh Lges 2E,2W (6)
Wed, 13th	Welsh Lge Premier (9)
Fri, 15th/	
Sat, 16th	Celtic League (7)
Sat, 16th	Zurich Premiership (7)
	English Senior Cup Rd 3
	English Int & Jun Cups Rd 2
	Scottish Premiership 1-3 (8)
	Scottish Nat Lges (all divs) (5)
	All Ireland Leagues 1-3 (1)
	Welsh Lge Premier (10)
	Welsh Lge 1 (9)
	Welsh Lges 2E,2W (7)
Wed, 20th	Welsh Lge 1 (10)
Sat, 23rd	Heineken Cup (1)
	English Nat League 1 (7)
	English Nat League 2 (6)
	English Nat League 3 (5)
	English Leagues (12 teams) (6)
	English Leagues (10 teams) (5)
	Scottish Premiership 1-3 (9)
	Scottish Nat Lges (all divs) (6)
	All Ireland Leagues 1-3 (2)
	Welsh Lge Premier,1 (11)
	Welsh Lges 2E,2W (8)
Sat, 30th	Heineken Cup (2)
	English Nat League 1 (8)
	English Nat League 2 (7)
	English Nat League 3 (6)
	English Leagues (12 teams) (7)
	English Leagues (10 teams) (6)
	Scottish Cup Rd 1
	Lansdowne v Shannon
	(All Ireland League 1) (2)
	All Ireland Leagues 2,3 (3)
	Welsh Challenge Cup Rd 2
	Welsh Lge Premier (12)
	Welsh Lges 2E,2W (9)

NOVEMBER 2004

Wed, 3rd	Welsh Lge Premier (13)
Fri, 5th/	
Sun, 7th	Celtic League (8)
Sat, 6th	WALES v SOUTH AFRICA
	Zurich Premiership (8)
	English Nat League 3 (7)
	English Senior Cup Rd 4
	English Int & Jun Cups Rd 3
	Scottish Premiership 1-3 (10)
	Scottish Nat Lges (all divs) (7)
	All Ireland League 1 (3)
	All Ireland Leagues 2,3 (4)
Fri, 12th/	
Sun, 14th	Celtic League (9)
Sat, 13th	ENGLAND v CANADA
	SCOTLAND v JAPAN
	IRELAND v SOUTH AFRICA
	Zurich Premiership (9)
	English Nat League 1 (9)
	English Nat Leagues 2,3 (8)
	English Leagues (12 teams) (8)
	English Leagues (10 teams) (7)
	Welsh Lge Premier (14)
	Welsh Lge 1 (12)
	Welsh Lges 2E,2W (10)
Sun, 14th	Scottish Premiership 1-3 (11)
	Scottish Nat Lges (all divs) (8)
Wed, 17th	Welsh Lge Premier (15)
Thur, 18th	Welsh Lge 1 (13)
Fri, 19th/	
Sun, 21st	Celtic League (10)
Sat, 20th	ENGLAND v SOUTH AFRICA
	SCOTLAND v AUSTRALIA
	WALES v NEW ZEALAND
	IRELAND v UNITED STATES
	Zurich Premiership (10)
	English Nat League 1 (10)
	English Nat Leagues 2,3 (9)
	English Leagues (12 teams) (9)
	English Leagues (10 teams) (8)
Sun, 21st	Scottish Cup Rd 2
Fri, 26th/	
Sun, 28th	Celtic League (11)
Fri, 26th	WALES v JAPAN
Sat, 27th	ENGLAND v AUSTRALIA
	SCOTLAND v SOUTH AFRICA
	IRELAND v ARGENTINA
	Zurich Premiership (11)
	English Nat Leagues 2,3 (10)
	English Senior Cup Rd 5
	English Int & Jun Cups Rd 4
	Welsh Lge Premier (16)
	Welsh Lge 1 (14)
	Welsh Lges 2E,2W (11)
Sun, 28th	Scottish Premiership 1-3 (12)
	Scottish Nat Lges (all divs) (9)

DECEMBER 2004

Sat, 4th	BARBARIANS v NZ
	(prov; Twickenham)
	Heineken Cup (3)

	English Nat Leagues 1-3 (11)
	English Leagues (12 teams) (10)
	English Leagues (10 teams) (9)
	Scottish Premiership 1-3 (13)
	Scottish Nat Lges (all divs) (10)
	All Ireland League 1 (4)
	All Ireland Leagues 2,3 (5)
	Welsh Lge Premier (17)
	Welsh Lge 1 (15)
	Welsh Lges 2E,2W (12)
Tue, 7th	OXFORD v CAMBRIDGE
	(Twickenham)
Sat, 11th	Heineken Cup (4)
	English Nat Leagues 1-3 (12)
	English Leagues (12 teams) (11)
	English Leagues (10 teams) (10)
	Scottish Premiership 1-3 (14)
	Scottish Nat Lges (all divs) (11)
	All Ireland Leagues 2,3 (6)
	Welsh Lge Premier (18)
	Welsh Lge 1 (16)
	Welsh Lges 2E,2W (13)
Fri, 17th/	
Sat, 18th	Celtic League (12)
Sat, 18th	English Nat Leagues 2,3 (13)
	English Leagues (12 teams) (12)
	English Senior Cup Rd 6
	English Junior Cup Rd 5
	Scottish Premiership 1-3 (15)
	Scottish Nat Lges (all divs) (12)
	All Ireland League 1 (5)
	All Ireland Leagues 2,3 (7)
	Welsh Challenge Cup Rd 3
	Welsh Lges 2E,2W (14)
Tue, 21st	Welsh Lge 1 (17)
Wed, 22nd	Welsh Lge Premier (19)
Sun, 26th/	
Mon, 27th	Zurich Premiership (12)
	English Nat League 1 (13)
	Celtic League (13)
Thu, 30th	Welsh Lge Premier (20)

JANUARY 2005

Sat, 1st/	
Sun, 2nd	Celtic League (14)
Sat, 1st	Zurich Premiership (13)
	English Nat League 1 (14)
Sat, 8th	Heineken Cup (5)
	English Nat League 1 (15)
	English Nat Leagues 2,3 (14)
	English Leagues (12 teams) (13)
	English Leagues (10 teams) (11)
	Scottish Premiership 1-3 (16)
	Scottish Nat Lges (all divs) (13)
	All Ireland League 1 (6)
	All Ireland Leagues 2,3 (8)
	Welsh Lge Premier (21)
	Welsh Lge 1 (18)
	Welsh Lges 2E,2W (15)
Sat, 15th	Heineken Cup (6)
	English Nat League 1 (16)
	English Nat Leagues 2,3 (15)

	English Intermediate Cup Rd 5	Tue, 15th	Welsh Lge 1 (22)
	English Junior Cup Rd 6	Wed, 16th	Welsh Lge Premier (25)
	Scottish Premiership 1-3 (17)	Fri, 18th/	
	Scottish Nat Lges (all divs) (14)	Sun, 20th	Celtic League (17)
	Shannon v UC Dublin	Sat, 19th	Zurich Premiership (16)
	(All Ireland Lge 1) (6)		English Nat Leagues 1-3 (19)
	All Ireland Leagues 2,3 (9)		English Leagues (12 teams) (17)
	Welsh Lge Premier (22)		English Leagues (10 teams) (14)
	Welsh Lge 1 (19)		Scottish Premiership 1-3 (20)
	Welsh Lges 2E,2W (16)		Scottish Nat Lges (all divs) (17)
Fri, 21st/			All Ireland League 1 (10)
Sun, 23rd	Celtic League (15)		All Ireland Leagues 2,3 (13)
Sat, 22nd	English Senior Cup Q-finals		Welsh Challenge Cup Rd 5
	English Nat League 1 (17)		Welsh Lges 2E,2W (19)
	English Nat Leagues 2,3 (16)	Sun, 20th	Bective Rangers v Highfield,
	English Leagues (12 teams) (14)		Dolphin v UL Bohemian
	English Leagues (10 teams) (12)		(both All Ireland 2) (13)
	Scottish Premiership 1-3 (18)	Tue, 22nd	Welsh Lge Premier (26)
	Scottish Nat Lges (all divs) (15)	Wed, 23rd	Welsh Lge 1 (23)
	All Ireland League 1 (7)	Fri, 25th	Scotland v Italy (Under 21)
	All Ireland Leagues 2,3 (10)		France v Wales (Under 21)
	Welsh Challenge Cup Rd 4	Sat, 26th	SCOTLAND v ITALY
	Welsh Lges 2E,2W (17)		FRANCE v WALES
Fri, 28th/			Ireland v England (Under 21)
Sun, 30th	Celtic League (16)		Zurich Premiership (17)
Sat, 29th	Zurich Premiership (14)		English Nat Leagues 1-3 (20)
	English Nat League 1 (18)		English Leagues (12 teams) (18)
	English Nat Leagues 2,3 (17)		English Leagues (10 teams) (15)
	English Leagues (12 teams) (15)	Sun, 27th	IRELAND v ENGLAND
	English Leagues (10 teams) (13)		Scottish Cup Rd 3
	English Nat U20 C'ship starts		
	Scottish Premiership 1-3 (19)	**MARCH 2005**	
	Scottish Nat Lges (all divs) (16)	Tue, 1st	Leicester v Barbarians
	All Ireland League 1 (8)	Fri, 4th/	
	All Ireland Leagues 2,3 (11)	Sun, 6th	Celtic League (18)
	Welsh Lge Premier (23)	Sat, 5th	English Cups Semi-finals
	Welsh Lge 1 (20)		English Nat League 3 (21)
	Welsh Lges 2E,2W (18)		Scottish Premiership 1-3 (21)
Sun, 30th	UL Bohemian v Young Munster		All Ireland Leagues 2,3 (14)
	(All Ireland Lge 2) (11)		Welsh Lge Premier (27)
			Welsh Lge 1 (24)
FEBRUARY 2005			Welsh Lges 2E,2W (20)
Wed, 2nd	Welsh Lge Premier (24)	Wed, 9th	Welsh Lge Premier (28)
Fri, 4th	France v Scotland (Under 21)	Fri, 11th	Ireland v France (Under 21)
	Wales v England (Under 21)		England v Italy (Under 21)
Sat, 5th	WALES v ENGLAND	Sat, 12th	ENGLAND v ITALY
	FRANCE v SCOTLAND		IRELAND v FRANCE
	Italy v Ireland (Under 21)		Scotland v Wales (Under 21)
	Zurich Premiership (15)		Zurich Premiership (18)
	English Nat Leagues 2,3 (18)		English Nat Leagues 1,2 (21)
	English Leagues (12 teams) (16)		English Nat League 3 (22)
	All Ireland League 1 (9)		English Leagues (12 teams) (19)
	All Ireland Leagues 2,3 (12)		English Leagues (10 teams) (16)
Sun, 6th	ITALY v IRELAND (Rome)	Sun, 13th	SCOTLAND v WALES
Wed, 9th	Welsh Lge 1 (21)		Scottish Cup Q-finals
Fri, 11th	Italy v Wales (Under 21)	Wed, 16th	East Midlands v Barbarians
	Scotland v Ireland (Under 21)		(Mobbs Memorial Match;
Sat, 12th	ITALY v WALES (Rome)		Northampton)
	SCOTLAND v IRELAND		Welsh Lge Premier (29)
	England v France (Under 21)	Thu, 17th	Welsh Lge 1 (25)
	English Int & Jun Cups Q-finals	Fri, 18th/	
Sun, 13th	ENGLAND v FRANCE	Sun, 20th	Celtic League (19)

Fri, 18th	England v Scotland (Under 21)
	Ireland v Wales (Under 21)
	Italy v France (Under 21)
Sat, 19th	ENGLAND v SCOTLAND
	ITALY v FRANCE (Rome)
	WALES v IRELAND
	English Nat League 2 (22)
	English Nat League 3 (23)
Wed, 23rd	Welsh Lge 1 (26)
Fri, 25th/	
Sun, 27th	Celtic League (20)
Sat, 26th	Zurich Premiership (19)
	English Nat League 1 (22)
	Scottish Premiership 1-3 (22)
	Scottish Nat Lges (all divs) (18)
	All Ireland League 1 (11)
	All Ireland Leagues 2,3 (15)
	Welsh Challenge Cup Q-finals
	Welsh Lges 2E,2W (21)
Sun, 27th	Lansdowne v Buccaneers
	(All Ireland Lge 1) (11)
	UL Bohemian v Thomond
	(All Ireland Lge 2) (15)

APRIL 2005

Sat, 2nd	Heineken Cup Q-finals
	English Nat Leagues 1,2 (23)
	English Nat League 3 (24)
	English Leagues (12 teams) (20)
	English Leagues (10 teams) (17)
	Scottish Cups Semi-finals
	Welsh Lge Premier (30)
	Welsh Lge 1 (27)
	Welsh Lges 2E,2W (22)
Fri, 8th/	
Sun, 10th	Celtic League (21)
Sat, 9th	Zurich Premiership (20)
	English Nat Leagues 1,2 (24)
	English Nat League 3 (25)
	English Leagues (12 teams) (21)
	English Leagues (10 teams) (18)
	All Ireland League 1 (12)
	All Ireland Leagues 2,3 (16)
	Welsh Lge Premier (31)
	Welsh Lge 1 (28)
	Welsh Lges 2E,2W (23)
Wed, 13th	Army v RAF (TBA)
Fri, 15th/	
Sun, 17th	Celtic League (22)
Sat, 16th	English Cups Finals (Twickenham)
	Zurich Premiership (21)
	English Nat U20 C'ship Q-finals
	All Ireland League 1 (13)
	All Ireland Leagues 2,3 (17)
	Welsh Challenge Cup S-finals
	Welsh Lge Premier (32)
	Welsh Lges 2E,2W (24)
Wed, 20th	RAF v RN (Newbury)
Sat, 23rd	Heineken Cup Semi-finals
	English Nat Leagues 1,2 (25)
	English Nat League 3 (26)
	English Leagues (12 teams) (22)

	Welsh Lge Premier (33)
	Welsh Lge 1 (29)
	Welsh Lges 2E,2W (25)
Fri, 29th/	
Sun, 1st May	Celtic Cup Quarter-finals
Sat, 30th	Zurich Premiership (22)
	English Nat Leagues 1,2 (26)
	English Nat Lge 3, 12s & 10s
	Play-offs
	All Ireland Lges 1-3 Play-offs
	Semi-finals
	Scottish Cups Finals (Murrayfield)
	Welsh Lge Premier (34)
	Welsh Lge 1 (30)
	Welsh Lges 2E,2W (26)

MAY 2005

Fri, 6th/	
Sun, 8th	Celtic Cup Semi-finals
Sat, 7th	Zurich Premiership Semi-finals
	RN v The Army (Twickenham)
	English County C'ship Rd 1
	English Nat U20 C'ship S-finals
	All Ireland Lges 1-3 Play-offs
	Finals
	Welsh Challenge Cup Final
	(Cardiff)
Sat 14th or	
Sun, 15th	Celtic Cup Final
Sat, 14th	Zurich Premiership Final
	(Twickenham)
	English County C'ship Rd 2
Sat, 21st	Heineken Cup Final (Murrayfield)
	BARBARIANS v SCOTLAND or
	WALES (TBA)
	English County C'ship Rd 3
Wed, 25th	BARBARIANS v SCOTLAND or
	WALES (TBA)
Sat, 28th	English County C'ship Final
	English Nat U20 C'Ship Final
	(both Twickenham)
Sun, 29th	ENGLAND v BARBARIANS
	(Twickenham)

JUNE 2005

Sat, 4th	Bay of Plenty v Lions (Rotorua)
Wed, 8th	Taranaki v Lions (New Plymouth)
Sat, 11th	NZ Maori v Lions (Hamilton)
Wed, 15th	Wellington v Lions (Wellington)
Sat, 18th	Otago v Lions (Dunedin)
Tue, 21st	Southland v Lions (Invercargill)
Sat, 25th	NZ v LIONS (Christchurch)
Tue, 28th	Manawatu v Lions
	(Palmerston North)

JULY 2005

Sat, 2nd	NZ v LIONS (Wellington)
Sat, 9th	NZ v LIONS (Auckland)

NB: An extra match may be played on Tuesday or Wednesday, 5th or 6th July 2005, in Auckland.

Rugby's charity supporting disadvantaged children and young people

Mission Statement

Wooden Spoon aims to enhance the quality and
prospect of life for children and young persons in the
United Kingdom and Ireland who are presently
disadvantaged either physically, mentally or socially

Charity Registration No: 326691